Maya® 5
KillerTips

The hottest collection of cool tips and hidden secrets for Maya

Eric Hanson

with Eric Pender
and Erik Miller

Killer Tips series developed by Scott Kelby

PUBLISHER
Stephanie Wall

PRODUCTION MANAGER
Gina Kanouse

ACQUISITIONS EDITOR
Elise Walter

DEVELOPMENT EDITOR
Chris Zahn

SENIOR PROJECT EDITOR
Sarah Kearns

COPY EDITOR
Ben Lawson

INDEXER
Lisa Stumpf

PROOFREADER
Kristy Hart

COMPOSITION
Kim Scott

MANUFACTURING COORDINATOR
Dan Uhrig

COVER DESIGN AND CREATIVE CONCEPTS
Felix Nelson

MARKETING
Scott Cowlin
Tammy Detrich
Hannah Onstad Latham

PUBLICITY MANAGER
Susan Nixon

International Standard Book Number: 0-7357-1373-1

Library of Congress Catalog Card Number: 2003112025

Printed in the United States of America

First printing: December, 2003

08 07 06 05 04   7 6 5 4 3 2

Interpretation of the printing code: The rightmost double-digit number is the year of the book's printing; the rightmost single-digit number is the number of the book's printing. For example, the printing code 03-1 shows that the first printing of the book occurred in 2003.

Trademarks

Warning and Disclaimer

To the three girls, source of all things good in my world.

—ERIC HANSON

To my Mom, for life-long love, support, encouragement,

and inspiration to follow my dreams.

—ERICK MILLER

For all the future effects animators out there.

—ERIC PENDER

ABOUT THE AUTHOR

 **Eric Hanson** is a visual effects artist specializing in digital environments and effects for feature films. Originally an architect, he established early 3D visualization studios for some of the country's largest architectural firms, including The Callison Partnership in Seattle and Gensler in Los Angeles. An expanding interest in film led to a move into visual effects work, resulting in senior CG artist positions with leading visual effects houses Digital Domain, Sony Imageworks, Dream Quest Images, Walt Disney Feature Animation, and SimEx Digital Studios. His work can be seen in *Spider-Man*, *Cast Away*, *Hollow Man*, *Mission to Mars*, *Bicentennial Man*, *Fantasia 2000*, *Atlantis*, and *The Fifth Element*, as well as many large-format special-venue films worldwide.

Eric specializes in 3D work with Maya, RenderMan, and Shake, and is an active teacher of those packages. He has taught for several years, having instructed courses on advanced 3D techniques at SGI's Silicon Studio and Gnomon School of Visual Effects, and is currently leading a curriculum on visual effects at the University of Southern California's School of Cinema-TV. He frequently speaks and holds workshops at various trade shows and schools domestically, as well as in Japan, even though he is not sure what to eat while there.

Eric is a member of ACM/Siggraph and the Visual Effects Society and holds a professional degree in Architecture from the University of Texas at Austin. He is currently contributing to a remarkable upcoming summer blockbuster at Digital Domain in Los Angeles. He wishes he could sleep more.

Eric can be reached at his web site, **www.visuraimaging.com**.

Erick Miller is currently a Technical Director at Digital Domain, the Venice, California-based Academy Award-winning visual effects studio responsible for digital effects in recent blockbusters such as *The Time Machine*, *Lord of the Rings*, *X-Men*, and *Armageddon*.

Erick uses Maya and its robust 3d environment in his everyday responsibilities, writing many proprietary Maya API plug-ins and MEL scripts, rigging advanced character setups and complex deformation systems, as well as developing structured production pipelines for high-budget feature films and commercial projects that work between Maya and other software applications. To integrate Maya's powerful open architecture, he combines artistic knowledge with MEL scripting, Maya's API, other external programming languages (Perl, Tcl), and C/C++ APIs (RenderMan, OpenGL).

After wrapping up a Maya-based crowd animation pipeline for Roland Emerick's apocalyptic end-of-the-world feature film entitled *The Day After Tomorrow*, Erick has taken the position of Technical Director Team Lead on the feature, *I, Robot*—a huge CG character film based on the acclaimed science fiction novels by Isaac Asimov, rooted around a struggle between robotics and humanity.

Erick has been a Maya user since its inception at version 1.0, and has a BFA in Computer Graphics. He has also taught one of Alias's famed Maya Master Classes at Siggraph, as well as presented at Siggraph's Technical Sketches on Maya-based projects completed at Digital Domain. In addition, Erick is one of the co-authors of another recent Maya book, titled *Inside Maya 5* (New Riders, 2003).

Eric Pender has been creating 3D effects animation on feature films since 1996. He has worked on movies such as *Alien Resurrection*, *Batman and Robin*, *Hard Rain*, *Air Force One*, *Sphere*, *Gone in Sixty Seconds*, *Mission to Mars*, and *Kangaroo Jack*, as well as the opening sequence for *Wonderful World of Disney* on ABC. He started out working for Alias|Wavefront in Santa Barbara and specializing in Dynamation, which was the original dynamics package created by Wavefront. Dynamation was used as the framework for the dynamics package in Maya. Eric has been using Maya in production since the first version.

ACKNOWLEDGMENTS

Without rambling on endlessly like a weepy Oscar acceptance speech, I would like to briefly wish a warm thanks to many of those who laid the train tracks down in front of me or added coal to the engine along the way. First and foremost, much love must go to my beautiful wife, Kari, and our little love buckets, Taylor and Shelby. Kids are the perfect foil to the artificial world of computer graphics, getting you right back in touch with what everything is ultimately all about. 3D artists often mistake the world as one big rendering, and Kari constantly keeps me in check that it is indeed much more. She has endured my crazed and relentless obsession with CGI for many years with amazing tolerance and support. Kari, it has been noted by management and you are in line for a modest bonus soon! Or at least a lot of comp time at the beach.

Professionally, I have had many fellow adventurers on this train ride, but huge thanks go out to the truly supportive ones, like brother Bill Hanson of Apple Computer, FX animator extraordinaire Cody Harrington, and design maestro Joe Cordelle. I can attribute much of my success to their well-timed mutual prodding and encouragement. There have been numerous enjoyable fellow travelers along the way, such as Mark Lefitz, Alex Nijmeh, Pat Finley, Chris Nichols, Travis Price, Ben Procter, Chris Cunningham, John Goodman, Allen Yamashita, and Eric Beggs, where it all started. Much has been learned (and laughed) from all.

I would attribute my inspiration of my CG environmental work to sources in both the built and "unbuilt" worlds. In the world of architecture, I admire progressive designers like Santiago Calatrava and Steven Holl, as well as past masters like Antonio St' Elia and Louis Kahn. In the natural world, I find immense depth and beauty in the American West in locations like Zion National Park, Canyonlands National Park, and Big Bend National Park, not to mention innumerable other locations throughout the Colorado Plateau. These gems deserve our respect and defense for future generations.

Thanks go out to the quality team at New Riders, including Elise Walter, Chris Zahn, Jim Lammers, Garry Lewis, and Linda Bump. You all made the ride smooth and pleasurable. I had two great contributors for the book, Erick Miller and Eric Pender, covering two deeper areas in Maya that I choose wisely only to dogpaddle in: character animation and dynamics. Their expertise is unequalled, and they are fast on the road to being sanctioned "Maya Masters." Not to mention we are in the planning stage for an operatic tour as the "Three Erics"—look for show times near you. Thanks to Alias|Wavefront for developing such a massive product and uniting the tribes. I had two terrific tech editors who helped out greatly, Greg Berridge and Adrian Dimond. Lastly, great thanks go out to Scott Kelby for the Killer Idea of the *Killer Tips* series—onward and upward!

Then there is the inevitable thanks and love going out to my parents, who got the train out of the station and continue to support my constantly unfolding artistic path while moving down the tracks.

These reviewers contributed their considerable hands-on expertise to the entire development process for *Maya 5 Killer Tips*. As the book was being written, these dedicated professionals reviewed all the material for technical content, organization, and flow. Their feedback was critical to ensuring that *Maya 5 Killer Tips* fits our readers' need for the highest-quality technical information.

Greg Berridge is currently the head instructor of the Digital Character Animation program at Vancouver Film School. He is a certified Maya Instructor holding accreditation in several areas of Maya expertise. Greg has completed work for several local Vancouver companies, including Lorax International. He has also spent time teaching Maya to content creators at Mainframe Entertainment. Greg has completed work for the NIAC (NASA Institute for Advanced Concepts) on the international front. First and foremost an instructor, Greg has been teaching Maya since it arrived six years ago. In addition to his professional endeavors, Greg is also working as an independent producer and is currently developing several concepts for television and film. He is also an aspiring author, hoping to have his own book published soon on the intricacies of Maya. Above all else, he is engrossed in Maya and breathes 3D content creation at every possible moment.

Adrian Dimond is an animation director and visual effects supervisor who currently resides in Los Angeles. Recent clients include *The Anna Nicole Show*, Korn, Cherish Productions' film *Cherish* with Robin Tunney, 3DO's *Mad Trix*, and Mattel's *Max Steel*. Adrian began his computer studies at The School of the Art Institute of Chicago, where he also studied painting, sculpture, performance, digital audio, and video. "When I discovered the world of 3D, I realized that I could combine all aspects of time and fine arts in one medium," he says. In his spare time, Adrian enjoys doing Perl scripting and rebuilding the front end of his car. Adrian is a very active member of highend3d.com, where he shares his insights and 10 years of experience of working in the CG industry.

TABLE OF CONTENTS

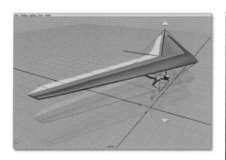

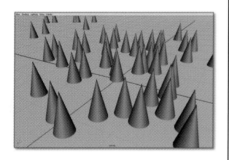

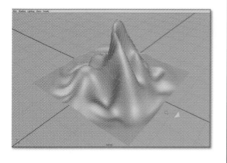

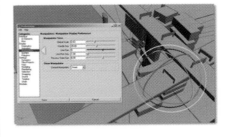

TABLE OF CONTENTS

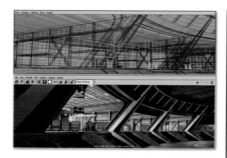

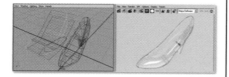

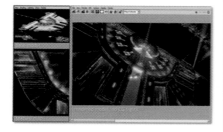

CHAPTER 5   78

Rags to Rendering

Getting a Grip on Shading

TABLE OF CONTENTS

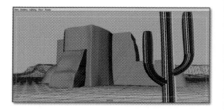

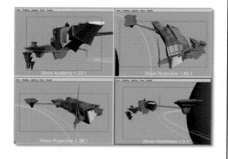

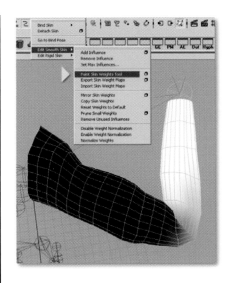

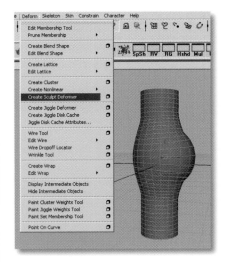

TABLE OF CONTENTS

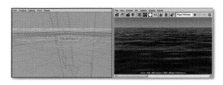

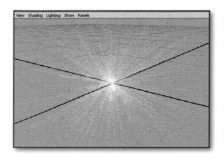

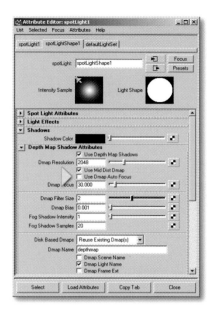

TELL US WHAT YOU THINK

As the reader of this book, you are the most important critic and commentator. We value your opinion and want to know what we're doing right, what we could do better, what areas you'd like to see us publish in, and any other words of wisdom you're willing to pass our way.

As an editor for New Riders Publishing, I welcome your comments. You can fax, email, or write me directly to let me know what you did or didn't like about this book—as well as what we can do to make our books stronger. When you write, please be sure to include this book's title, ISBN, and author, as well as your name and phone or fax number. I will carefully review your comments and share them with the author and editors who worked on the book.

Please note that I cannot help you with technical problems related to the topic of this book, and that due to the high volume of email I receive, I might not be able to reply to every message.

Fax: 317-428-3280

Email: elise.walter@newriders.com

Mail: Elise Walter
         Acquisitions Editor
         New Riders Publishing
         800 East 96th Street, 3rd Floor
         Indianapolis, IN 46240 USA

FOREWORD

Maya 5 Killer Tips
Edited by Scott Kelby

Welcome to *Maya 5 Killer Tips*. As Editor for the Killer Tips series, I can't tell you how excited and truly gratified I am to see this concept of creating a book that is cover-to-cover nothing but tips, extend from my original book (*Photoshop Killer Tips*) into *Maya 5 Killer Tips*.

The idea for this series of books came to me when I was at the bookstore looking through the latest Photoshop books on the shelf. I found myself doing the same thing to every book I picked up: I'd turn the page until I found a paragraph that started with the word "Tip." I'd read the tip, then I'd keep turning until I found another sidebar tip. I soon realized I was hooked on tips, because I knew that if I were writing the book that's where I'd put all my best material. Think about it: If you were writing a book, and you had a really cool tip, an amazing trick, or an inside secret or shortcut, you wouldn't bury it among hundreds of paragraphs of text. No way! You'd make it stand out: You'd put a box around it, maybe put a tint behind it, and if it was really cool (and short and sweet), you'd get everybody's attention by starting with the word "Tip!"

That's what got me thinking. Obviously, I'm not the only one who likes these tips, because almost every software book has them. There's only one problem: There's never *enough* of them. And I thought, "Wouldn't it be great if there were a book that was nothing but those cool little tips?" (Of course, the book wouldn't actually have sidebars, since what's in the sidebars would be the focus: nothing but cool shortcuts, inside secrets, slick ways to do the things we do everyday, but faster—and more fun— than ever!) That was the book I really wanted, and thanks to the wonderful people at New Riders, that's the book they let me write (along with my co-author and good friend Felix Nelson). It was called *Photoshop Killer Tips*, and it became an instant bestseller because Felix and I were committed to creating something special: A book where every page included yet another tip that would make you nod your head, smile, and think "Ahhh, so that's how they do it."

> **TIP**
>
> *If you were writing a book, and you had a really cool tip, an amazing trick, or an inside secret or shortcut, you wouldn't bury it among hundreds of paragraphs of text. You'd make it stand out: You'd put a box around it, maybe put a tint behind it, and if it was really cool (and short and sweet), you'd get everybody's attention by starting with the word "Tip!"*

If you've ever wondered how the pros get twice the work done in half the time, it's really no secret: They do everything as efficiently as possible. They don't do *anything* the hard way. They know every timesaving shortcut, every workaround, every speed tip, and as such they work at full speed all the time. They'll tell you, when it comes to being efficient, and when it comes to staying ahead of the competition: Speed Kills!

Well, what you're holding in your hand is another Killer Tips book:
A book packed cover-to-cover with nothing but those cool little sidebar tips (without the sidebars). Eric Hanson has captured the spirit and flavor of what a Killer Tips book is all about. I can't wait for you to get into it, so I'll step aside and let him take the wheel, because you're about to get faster, more efficient, and have more fun in Maya 5 than you ever thought possible.

Have fun and enjoy the ride!

All my best,

Scott Kelby, Series Editor

INTRODUCTION

Not for the Faint of Heart

3D artists have it tough. They have to wade through seemingly endless amounts of technical minutia from dreary manuals, off-the-shelf books thicker than the yellow pages in a grimy Manhattan phone booth, and well-intentioned but often awkward online tutorials. Then they navigate bleary-eyed through the endless layers of cryptic commands in their applications, wrestling such terms as "Directed Acyclic Graph," "Non-Rational Uniform B-Spline," and "Non-Manifold Topology." If you can recite the meaning of these terms without forethought, you have already been there! We endure this toil just to satisfy our implacable creative urges to muster up fascinating imagery out of the deep well of technology. 3D animation and rendering is certainly the high ground of computer graphics, pushing one's capacity for technical concepts and jargon to the limit. And, like your grandfather in his youth, mythically trudging through miles of snow making his way to school, we actually LIKE it that way! So, what better reason than to create a book that assembles concise technical tips to speed understanding of the terms, accelerate your workflow to superhuman speeds, and peer into techniques professionals use daily in the visual effects field? When I learned of Scott Kelby's *Killer Tips* series, I recognized that it would be an instant fit in the 3D CGI* world, like beer and pretzels, or in our case, hot pockets and programmers.

Why Maya?

Maya has had an interesting ride into the annals of CGI history in the last few years. It has pounded its way like Mike Tyson into the forefront of professional 3D, and is now considered the standard for 3D work at most of the major visual effects facilities, such as Acme Animagraphics and Industrial FX R Us. Seriously though, it has swept the field, and if there is anything good about that, it is that artists can now carry their expertise and well-earned training with them as they drift from project to project, like the best migrant beanfield workers.

Maya began life as three competing products (Alias, Wavefront, and TDI) that Silicon Graphics had the good sense to purchase and then fuse, Frankenstein-like, into the ultimate über-3D software. Think of it as Einstein's Grand Unification Theory applied to 3D. Or dogs and cats happily romping together. Or Steve Jobs and Bill Gates taking a buddy road trip through the southwestern desert together. In any case, it consolidated many of the separately evolved features that 3D artists had grown envious of. It reduced the prevalent 3D application "camp" mentality somewhat and joined the tribes.

But what secured the success of Maya in the high-end world was that it was the first 3D package to "open the hood" for standard users, allowing amateur

---

* First "TLA," or three-letter acronym, that 3D artists seem to prefer for basic conversation to each other; in this case, "computer graphics imagery."

weekend mechanics (non-programmers) to rummage around in the engine and transmission. So rather than offering an ultimately dead-end tunnel of predetermined GUI* commands, Maya reveals all command structure in text format, allowing clever custom tools to be created (or bumbling stupid ones). Some hardcore Maya users balk at using a GUI at all and type everything. The same crowd would probably prefer punch cards if they were still around, but the option does exist.

Maya also delivers cutting-edge performance in most of the areas it is known for, such as extensive modeling, rich character animation, highly developed dynamic simulation, and a multitude of deformations, as well as offering unique technology like fluid effects, cloth simulation, 3D paint effects, and non-linear animation. Ultimately, Maya has become the "Swiss army knife" of visual effects. Of course, Swiss army knives are not exactly sleek and are fairly cumbersome, and Maya can be seen similarly. Thus, a good understanding is needed to "tame the beast" and coax it into doing your bidding. Alias's early advertising campaign involving a circus lion tamer is not too far off in that regard.

Is This Book for Me?

Absolutely. This book is designed for the advancing intermediate Maya artist, but it will offer gems to all levels. It is amazing how many Maya techniques fall through the cracks for even the most seasoned, jaded 3D guru. The fact is, no one artist can know ALL there is in Maya, so most hunker down into one area or another. Therefore, beginners will find it valuable to clear up some of the arcane mystery of the program, intermediates will use it to add to their growing bevy of techniques, and old dogs will learn a few new tricks to polish off their expertise. Some power users say it is ALL about the tricks and guard them ferociously. So, if you use Maya at all, breathe air, have ten fingers, ten toes, and one head, it probably is a book for you. Not that you HAVE to have those requirements, of course.

Can I Get a Job Working with Steven Spielberg or Jim Cameron After I Read It?

Sure, why not? Stranger things have happened in Hollywood. Steven Spielberg started as a squatter in a studio lot, and Jim Cameron was a truck driver. I would say with that in mind, you could certainly make your mark in Hollywood, armed with the aid of *Maya Killer Tips*. One of the truly great aspects of the visual effects field is that ultimately it is only about your talent. Well, sure, there are SOME power lunches involved, but mastering a difficult package like Maya is a surefire and road-tested route to contribute to the history of the silver screen, and not a bad 8–5 gig if you ask me. Or there's always the beanfield….

* Another TLA; in this case, "graphic user interface," affectionately known as "gooey."

Deciphering the Hieroglyphics

One's first reaction to opening a session of Maya might be similar to that of an archeologist unearthing an ancient Mayan stone calendar in a remote

Deciphering the Hieroglyphics

unearthing the secrets of the maya

Yucatan jungle. Carefully wiping the dust and pulling the vines away, one knows that the codified icons and glyphs mean something of importance, but what? Similarly, Maya's workflow is not easily deduced from its outward appearance, as it contains many secrets waiting to be discovered by the intrepid and dedicated explorer. In spite of its arcane appearance, however, it is ultimately designed for a fast and efficient workflow. This chapter will introduce you to some of the little known ways around the program that should speed your productivity and add to your magical aura as a 3D guru. When mastered, you too can feel like a high priest of some secret fraternal order, but luckily without requiring the silly fez hats and robes. You might feel an urge to parade around in miniature cars, though....

HEY, SPLIT IT

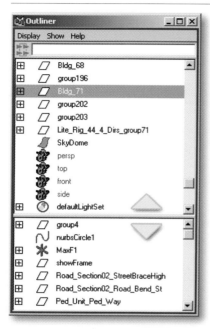

One downfall of having everything expressed as nodes in Maya is that the process of selecting them can get quite tedious. The outliner is the preferred method for speed of selection, but what if you are trying to parent a node at the top of the list to one buried thousands of nodes below? Dragging a node to enable scrolling down could take you longer than your lunch break. One often-overlooked enhancement made to the Outliner window is the capability to pull up the bottom edge to split it into two portions, for drag-and-drop speed nirvana….

    USE THE FIELDS, LUKE

Selecting is one of the key Maya skills in life, like learning not to spill on yourself during meals. For those unruly cases where you have 5,000 elements called fooThing0001 through fooThing5000, you could lasso all successive nodes in the Outliner, but it is much more expedient to type this bit of MEL scripting in the Script window: `select "fooThing*"`. Quicker still is to type the same phrase sans the " " into the selection entry field in the main menu strip for ultra-deluxe picking speed!

STRAWBERRY OUTLINER FIELDS FOREVER

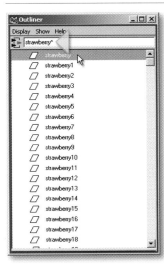

Another great place to practice your fields is the unnamed entry bar at the top of the Outliner. Rather than tediously hunting for a particular name nested in an extensive list of nodes, type in wildcards of your choice to limit what the Outliner will now return back to you. Hit the button to the left of the field to return back to the full listing.

   ### TRASH THAT PREF

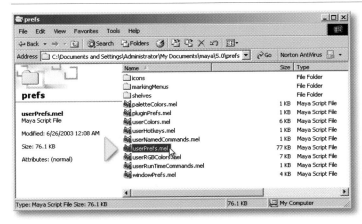

Even though we want to believe that Maya can do no wrong as a pinnacle of software perfection, every now and then its behavior will get unruly and corrupted, not unlike teenagers. You can perform your own style of troubled teen intervention by deleting the userPrefs.mel file that resides in your maya/5.0/prefs folder in the Documents and Settings folder on your drive. You will lose your marking menus and hotkeys by doing so, but it is a small price to pay to help steer Maya down a productive, non-self-destructive path in life.

FIELD OPERATORS ARE STANDING BY

Here is a hot tip for those who have had trouble with basic arithmetic past grade school. Let's say that random transform values are set in the attribute fields of an object, but you are asked to alter it by 147% (150% would be too easy in this case). Rather than take time to break out what my very "old school" engineering professor used to call those new "electronic hand-held calculators", you can highlight the field(s) in question and use *=147 to magically multiply all the values by that amount. Other arithmetic operators such as +=, −=, and /= can all be used to avoid that hand-held marvel of technology!

NUDGE 'EM

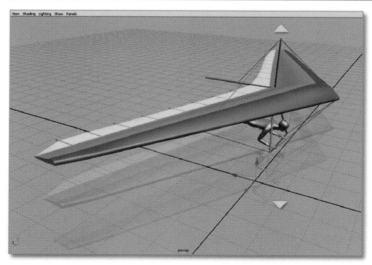

Moving objects around in 3D space quickly is usually not too tough, but carefully adjusting small values to hone it in can be. Rather than fumble with grossly sensitive transform handles, press Alt and then your Up/Down/ Left/Right arrow keys to perform surgically precise 1-pixel nudges on your elements— the closest we come to performing delicate brain surgery in Maya. Bear in mind, this will affect all three axes in the Perspective view, while the Up/Down and Left/Right are axially bound in the Orthographic views.

ANNOTATE AWAY

One useful recently added feature you may not have explored is the capability to append text strings to objects in your scene, a virtual post-it note for your working views. Pick an object, and then choose Create, Annotation to automatically group a target locator and text field node to it, with text editable in the attributeShape node in the Attribute Editor. The text will orient to proper screen space in each view, giving you the ability to clutter up your scene with random daily motivational affirmations or perhaps even useful technical information.

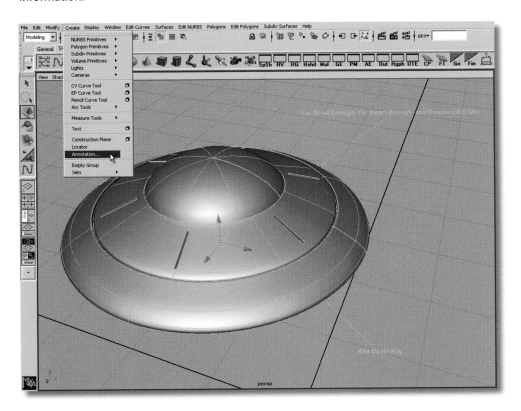

OUTLINER REVEALED AT LAST

Upon selecting an object, one speedy way to locate it in the Outliner under an impossibly deep hierarchy is to choose Outliner, Display, Reveal Selected, whereupon the node is uncovered from the murky depths and revealed in all its blazing glory for all to see.

GET IN LINE, LOWLY VERTICES

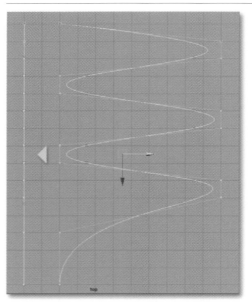

Here is a little gem for those cases when a succession of CVs or vertices must align in an axis without losing other alignments. Pick the multiple points, choose Transform with the "w" key, and then click on the shaft of the axis to align to. Make sure that Retain Component Spacing is unchecked in the Move Transform options, and then use a snap hotkey such as grid snap (x) to click somewhere, pulling all renegade points to line up like the Music City Rockettes. If they start a chorus line serenade at that point, consider shutting down and taking the rest of the day off.

SCRUB IT

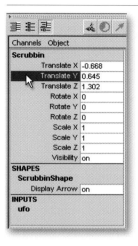

No, I am not talking about scrubbing your workspace clean, although I have seen enough CG artists' and programmers' environments to know that is not a bad idea. I am referring to the handy but unseen way to scrub values interactively in either the Attribute Editor or Channel Box. In the AE, click in an attribute field and use the Ctrl key and left mouse button to push values up or down on the fly. Try the middle mouse button for a faster response time. Even handier is clicking on the attribute name to highlight it in the Channel Box and then scrubbing your middle mouse button anywhere in a panel view for a true interactive experience. Very handy when the transform handle is hard to distinguish from a dense wireframe behind it.

TUMBLE CAMP

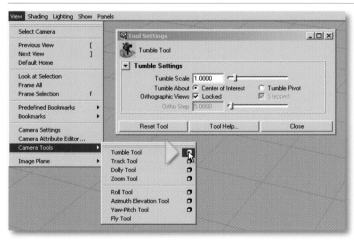

Tumbling through life with default settings is fine for most people, but you know you are not one of them. You enjoy being out on the edge. For you, pushing the envelope of tumbling is where you want to be. Rather than use the default Alt key and left mouse button, invoke the Tumble Tool options under View Panel Menu, View, Camera Tools, Tumble Tool <options>. First, turn the Tumble Scale from 1 to, dare I say it, one more than 10, 11! Unbridled speed is now yours, and you will dazzle anyone who watches the spectacle. Another nugget is to enable stepped orthographic panel tumbling, normally reserved only for Olympian athletes, but available for the fearless Maya artist who dares tread there.

GOT SPREADSHEETS?

If you were ever envious of financial wizards manipulating great sums of wealth on spread-sheets all day long, look no further. You, the Maya *artiste*, have had your own little spread-sheet in Maya the whole time. It may not make you financially independent, but it will certainly prevent gray hair formation. You can use it to alter a collection of entities from geometry to lights to shaders, preventing the dreaded tedium of manual node-to-node updating. For example, pick a large array of point lights and go to Main Menu, Window, Attribute Spread Sheet to witness all the attributes made available to you in cell format. Now alter a column by clicking in a column header in the top row, punch in a value, and adjust all intensities simultaneously. Not seeing ALL the attributes, such as those in the shape nodes? Simply pickwalk down using the down arrow key once to view all shape nodes' attributes.

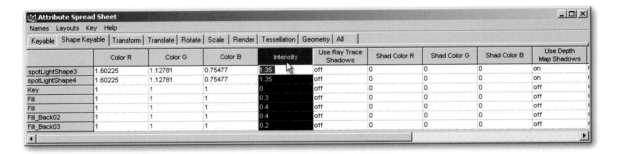

   ### PANEL HOPPING

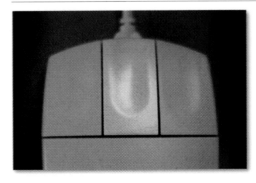

You may have noticed that when you select a new panel by clicking in it while having an element selected, the panel becomes active, but you lose the selection in the process, not unlike dropping your groceries while leaving the store. An easier alternative than clicking the panel menu bar is to click in the panel using the middle mouse button, which keeps hold of your selected goods, changes the panel, and saves face in public.

IT'S THE RIGHT THING TO DO

Many beginning Maya users will fail to notice things not immediately obvious to them, such as their noses. Beyond that, they may not notice that many of Maya's controls are set up to take advantage of the right mouse button extensively. For example, right-clicking and holding over an object yields a selection mask menu, over the timeline yields all commands relevant to playback and some Graph Editor commands, and over any attribute field yields a full set of keyframe commands. Right-click menus are spread well throughout the package in many more areas, so right-click with abandon!

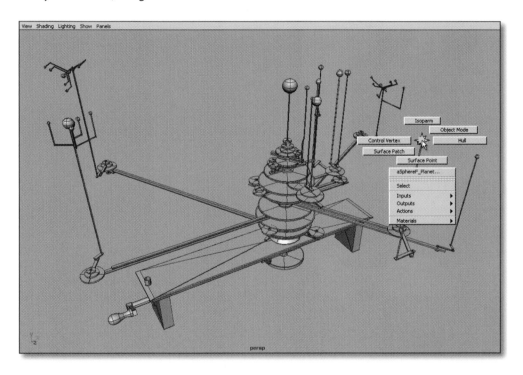

DRAG-DROP FEVER

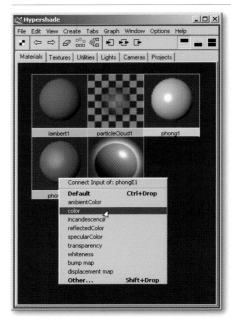

Another implementation that may not be obvious in Maya is the drag-drop of node upon node. One classic use of this is to drag one node over another in the Outliner window to parent it below what it is dragged onto. Conversely, you can drag out of a hierarchy into open space in the Outliner to unparent the node. With the Multilister or Hypershade open, drag a Shader Icon directly over some geometry to assign. If you want a new shader created, no need to create it first; drag a shader type from the Create Render Node window on the geometry to assign and create in one step. While working in shader networks, drag various shading nodes onto each other to make connections. Color is the default connection if Ctrl is used, but if you need the Connection Editor, try Shift drag-drop.

LAST ACTION HERO

A very handy key to use when modeling curves or surfaces is the "y" key, which Alias mysteriously calls the "non-sacred tool." Having little to do with anything heretical, it simply completes your tool and resets for another session. For example, drawing a curve is performed by placing many points successively. Rather than use the Return key to complete it and then have to hit the Curve tool icon again, place the last point, hit the "y" key, and you are ready to draw the start point of the next curve. Quite a time-saver for big tracing or curve-generation sessions.

LAST COMMAND HERO

Here is a great little-used key that can really speed up modeling: the "g" or "G" key. If you are creating multiples or doing repetitions of modeling tasks, this is for you. For example, create a primitive cone, move it off of world origin, and then hit "g" to create another. A more interesting variation is "G," where the last action is performed wherever the cursor is located. Hit "G" repeatedly while moving the mouse about and quickly create a forest of cone trees! Create a more complex forest by writing a MEL script that creates a branching tree based on a random seed, and the simple "G" key can quickly rough out a complex environment.

MARQUEE ZOOMING

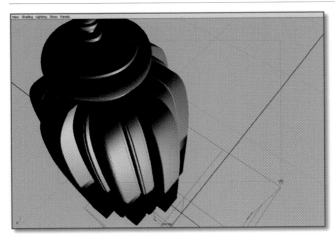

The dolly command works well for navigating in and out of objects. Alternately, the "f" key fits to a small object, which essentially zooms in. But when you might want to frame a given range or dolly out at a significant speed, try the marquee-zoom trick. Press Ctrl and Alt while dragging a region from upper left to lower right. The framed region is now zoomed into. To reverse out, drag from lower right to upper left.

GESTURAL TRANSFORMS

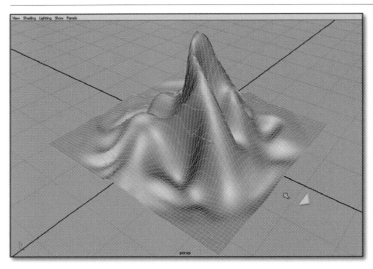

Not a form of pantomime as it might sound, gestural transforms are a somewhat forgotten feature developed early on in Maya. Normally, to transform an object, one would use the transform handles or virtual slider described in the earlier "Scrub It" tip in this chapter. A speedier and seemingly more magical technique is to select the object, press the "w" key to enable transforms, and then hold Shift down and use the middle mouse button to gesturally slide the object along an imaginary axis that is roughly aligned to X, Y, or Z. The movement is constrained to the nearest axis, so one can move the object in 3 axes very quickly without selecting any additional commands.

INCREMENTAL SAVES

Saving is one of the areas that every Maya user has wished he or she had done more often at times. Inevitably, either because of a power outage, BSD*, or file corruption, loud groaning can be emitted from Maya artists, sounding like something from a wildlife documentary. One way to prevent this is to use the Incremental Save feature in Maya, found in File, Save Options. Incremental Saves creates an indexed series of backup files during your basic save, enabling you to retrieve an earlier uncorrupted or more successful version.

The classic Windows system failure affectionately known as the "Blue Screen of Death."

ROTATION SNAPPING

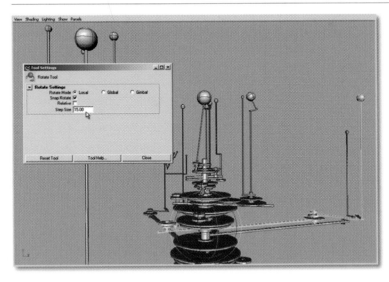

Often when manipulating objects, you need to rotate in fixed increments, especially for architectural situations. In the past you had to tediously input a relative offset rotation in the Field Entry Box. With a recent addition to v5.0, you can double-click the Rotate icon on the sidebar, select Snap Rotate and Step Size, and then effectively ball and detent the rotation of your objects. Very helpful when repeating actions for a model.

CLIP IT, CLIP IT GOOD

Maya's defaults are set up primarily for working with objects larger than a breadbox and smaller than a house, like characters or vehicles. When working with larger items, such as Manhattan Island, the default camera clipping can hide much of your model. Going to each camera's Attribute Editor can be tedious, so use this bit of MEL to expand that default clipping:

```
setAttr "frontShape.farClipPlane" 100000;
setAttr "sideShape.farClipPlane" 100000;
setAttr "topShape.farClipPlane" 100000;
setAttr "perspShape.farClipPlane" 100000;
```

This can be a handy shelf item to have, so look in Chapter 2's "Do-It-Yourself Shelving" tip for shelf-creation advice

  TOOLS VERSUS ACTIONS

Maya was designed with basic precepts in mind, not unlike the U.S. Constitution. One of these base concepts is that *tools* or *actions* can influence nodes. Many users never learn the difference and thus are surprised by some behavior in the package. The fundamental difference is that a *tool* is active and accepting of input until completed or until the next command is chosen. Examples of tools are the Selection Arrow or any of the Curve tools. Tool options are generally accessed by double-clicking the tool. An *action* is more of a single-shot event made upon a selection, like Lofting or Set Key. Keep in mind that actions often are dictated by the order of the selections, like Edit Curves, Cut Curves. Action options are accessed through the square option box in the menus. These options can be left open to try different settings, unlike tool options. Note that in Window, Settings/Preferences, Preferences under Modeling you can change the behavior of the modeling tools to act as either Tools or Actions, allowing Maya to act like previous software from which you may be transitioning.

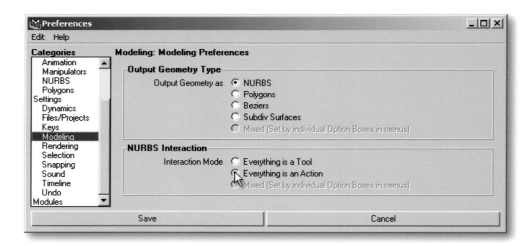

RMB SELECTION MENUS

One of the classic "speed traps" in Maya involves having to continually go to the Selection Mask Menus to choose component level entities, such as CVs or vertices. A workhorse of efficient Maya workflow is the selection mask assigned to the right mouse button. As you pass the mouse over an object, right-click for selection menus that give context-sensitive selection depending on geometry type (NURBS or polys). On top of enabling an easy pick of components, you can select the object from there, change display type, assign or inspect materials, and even invoke the 3D paint command for a little touch-up work. Now hold Ctrl and right-click, and selection Grow and Shrink commands are made available for the truly lazy and/or speed-driven.

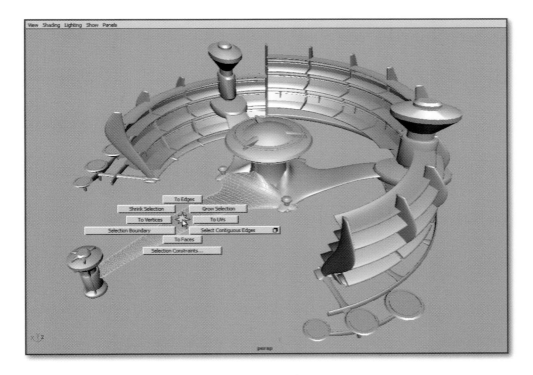

Taming the Beast

3D artists love to gaze at explicit pictures of aircraft interiors, particularly cockpits. Endless banks of needles, gauges, and knobs elicit drool and envy in

Taming the Beast
customizing your interface

most Maya users. Why, you ask? Simply because working in Maya is a lot like flying a 767, albeit a lot lower and slower. We gear heads enjoy rich interfaces with lots of sliders and buttons to push, just to see what happens. I would venture to say that software preference is based primarily on interface preference. So, with that in mind, Maya users enjoy having a lack of boundaries in their software with respect to both function and interface. Alias wisely recognized this fact, and they built what is probably the most customizable interface of any 3D package. This chapter could easily comprise a book in itself, but I will point out some of the key ways to personalize your interaction with Maya. But be careful, Maya artists can become obsessive in their customization of their GUIs, not unlike some cars with fuzzy dice and curb feelers.

START UP YOUR OWN IMAGE

The first thing we can change is coincidentally the first thing you see in Maya—the startup screen. This is nothing more than free promo for Alias, but you are welcome to replace it with your own little ad campaign, from your kid pictures to your last rendering. Doing so, however, takes a bit of mucking around with some internal files. First, locate the file MayaRes.dll in the bin directory of Maya's install location. Copy this file as a backup, and then use a resource-editing program, such as Restorator, to open it with. Locate MAYASTARTUPIMAGE.XPM.bmp and save this embedded file to disk. Next, edit away in Photoshop, maintaining original pixel dimensions. Now, replace the original with your revised image in the resource-editing program and restart Maya. Now you, too, can have a fully globally illuminated, subsurface scattered, photon mapped, and high-dynamic range lit logo of Maya upon startup, which is sure to be the envy of all your neighbors on the block.

TRUE GESTURAL MARKING MENUS

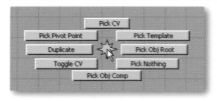

The Hotbox is a wonderful invention in Maya. Another wonderful invention is Marking Menus. Unfortunately, they don't play too well together, as the true speed attainable in Marking Menus is hampered somewhat by having to call the Hotbox first. If you are not wed to the use of the Hotbox (some are, some aren't), you can disable it by calling it up with the spacebar, and then selecting Hotbox Controls, Hotbox Styles, Center Zone Only. Now its display is disabled, enabling direct access to gestural behavior from the Marking Menus. To use a Marking Menu gesturally, first hold the spacebar and one of the three buttons on the mouse and make a quick snapping motion in a cardinal direction, which enables the command without ever having to see the label appear from it. After you are used to this way of working, you can never go back, effectively crippling you when you do go back to normal GUI methods, such as helping students or fellow workers at their machines. Lastly, if you do want the Hotbox back, just press Alt-m.

COLOR MY WORLD

Color schemes are another popular way to totally personalize your interface. Color modification in Maya is practically unlimited and can range from a subtle study in tonal design minimalism to an appearance that would make a circus clown happy. Color changes can be made to virtually any entity, from wireframes to background colors. Global color preferences can be modified in Window, Settings/Preferences, Colors, which is separated into General, Active, and Non-active entity categories. The color of individual objects can be set in a multitude of ways. First, select an object, and then go to Display, Wireframe Color for a basic selection from an indexed palette. Next, open the Attribute Editor on the object and locate Object Display, Drawing Overrides. Here, you can change color on a per-object basis. Note that this same override is located on the shape node as well. Lastly, on the MEL side, an object can be selected and changed with this command: `color -ud [ color #]`, where `color #` refers to system IDs of an indexed palette. Finally, to quickly undo any color of an active element, simply type `color`. Doesn't get much easier than that.

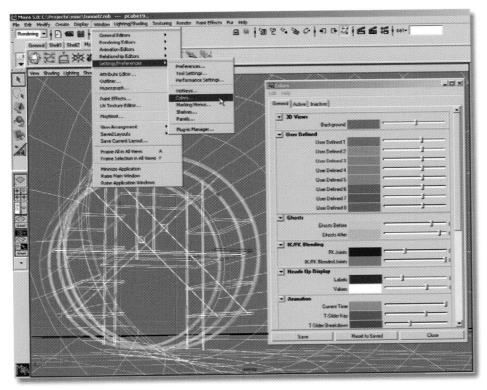

DO-IT-YOURSELF SHELVING

Shelves are a truck stop on the road to total customization of Maya— they offer easy setup and access, but they don't quite offer the high performance of a Marking Menu or Hotkey. Maya provides a few shelves that suffice for a starting point, but feel free to delete them and build your own. Use the Shelf Editor to create a new shelf, and then hold Shift-Control-Alt as you invoke a command to add it to the active shelf. You can then MMB drag them for reordering, inter-shelf mixing, or a one-way trip to the Trash icon at the far right. Remember, shelves are saved in the C:\Documents and Settings*user*\My Documents\maya\5.0\ prefs\shelves directory for easy emailing or transport between job locations. Often, a project-based shelf will be made for a team containing a suite of custom tools for the tasks required. Lastly, the Shelf Tabs consume a small but wasteful strip of screen real estate, so turn them off with the black down arrow pull-down at the far left of the shelf and use the selecting button just above it to alternate between tabs.

   ## SHELF ICON DECOR

The truly hardcore custom Maya GUI zealots will want to detail their shelf appearances with their own graphic icons and decor. Consider this the interior decoration of Maya. To revise the standard command icon or put fancy renders on MEL script shelf buttons, go to the Shelf Editor, and then choose the Shelf tab to pick the shelf you want to customize. Next, choose the command from Shelf Contents, and then press the Change Image button below. Note the resolution is fixed at 32×32 pixels, and the formats are limited to .xpm, .bmp, and .dib. One possibility is to split a single image into a sequential series of icons that form an image, perhaps of your favorite soap opera star or hair band.

CUSTOM MARKING MENUS—THE BOMB

Perhaps one of the most useful customization modes you can create to speed your work-flow is that of setting up a custom Marking Menu. Rooted in MEL scripts, they can be set up for a specific set of tasks for a project or used as the backbone in your workflow. To create one, first create Shelf items of the commands you would like to add. Use "Echo All Commands" in the Script Editor to help display these commands in the Script Editor. When highlighted and MMB dragged to a shelf, open the Marking Menu Editor in Main Menu, Window, Settings/Preferences, Marking Menus. When there, use Create Marking Menu to MMB drag your newly created shelf commands to a rosette layout, and then save to the Marking Menu directory in your Maya\5.0\prefs folder in the Documents and Settings folder on your drive. Next, assign each Menu to the Hotbox Center or Hotkey Editor. I prefer dis-abling the Hotbox and setting them in the Center zone, but it is entirely a personal call. For example, highlight a Menu, choose Center Hotbox Region, and put each respective Menu on L, M, or R buttons. Now glory and revel in amazing speed gains, never needing to hunt down your commonly used commands again. Other options for the truly power hungry are to have multiple sets assigned to Hotbox Quadrants or multiple Hotkeys. The danger in all this, of course, is that you will be quite helpless when working on a machine not configured for your soon-to-be neurally embedded configuration.

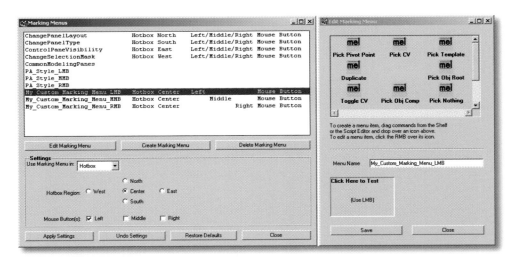

   MY VERY OWN ATTRIBUTES

Maya has so many attributes that you might wonder why anyone would want more. The reason is simply this: One of Maya's most powerful features is the capability to add GUI as needed. You can create custom interfaces to serve very specific tasks that might need isolating into their own menu area for ease of use. You can also extend typical attributes. As a common example, a character rigger might provide the skeleton IK setup and then provide a series of attribute sliders that control a very unique animation that the character might contain. Rather than having to type rotations in XYZ in various default named nodes, the animator might find "ArmSwing" or "ExtendTentacle." If only the 1950's pulp sci-fi's had it this good! To set up a simple example, create a sphere, rename it "Orb" in the Channel Box, and then choose Attribute Editor, Attributes, Add Attributes. Call the Attribute Name "Orb_Spin" and select Add. Now right-click on the Rotate Y field and choose Expressions. In the Expression Editor, type `Orb.rotateY = Orb_Spin;` and complete it. Now look for Orb_Spin in the Extra Attributes of the Attribute Editor and take it for a spin (sorry). Custom attributes are typically rigged with expressions such as this, so brushing up on them won't hurt.

CLICK, DRAG, SELECT!

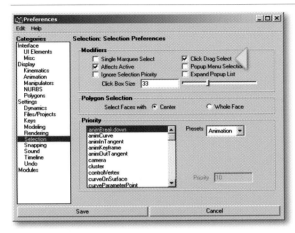

Sounding a bit like a command barked from a high school gym coach, this is actually a nice way to speed up your workflow if you are moving a lot of elements around. Typically, you first must pick an object and then choose a transform tool on it to move, but this enables a single step for picking many objects in a row without having to re-invoke the tool action. Turn on this little-known feature by checking Window, Settings/Preferences, Preferences, Settings, Selection, Click-Drag-Select.

Now move and arrange, say, a group of bowling pins quickly by clicking and dragging one by one in succession.

 TO GUI OR NOT TO GUI?

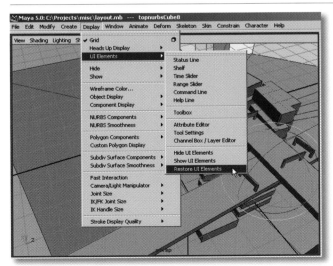

For the ultimate GUI (or lack thereof), some Maya enthusiasts turn off all the GUI elements and operate strictly with the panel view and Hotbox. Although this is not a scientifically verified technique for attracting the opposite sex, it can certainly invoke awe in casual bystanders. To turn all GUI elements off, go to Display, UI elements, Hide UI Elements. Note this option is also available by right-clicking in the knurled-looking Stow buttons in each UI component. To restore them, go back to Display, UI elements, Restore UI Elements.

    MASSIVE OR TINY MANIPULATION

Transform manipulators come at a default size, but they can be changed on the fly when they become hard to discern by wireframes or various displays. Simply use the + or – keys to scale them up to superhuman scale or down to petite sizes. This can also be handy when a finer degree of manipulation is required temporarily because the larger size can enable finer indexing. To set them at a fixed custom size every session, go to Window, Settings/ Preferences, Preferences, Display, Manipulators, and set thicker lines, global sizing, and so on.

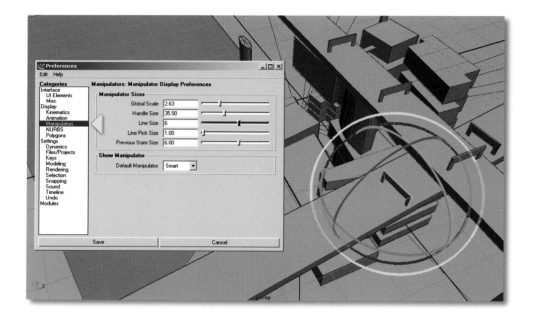

    PICK NOTHING, NOTHING AT ALL

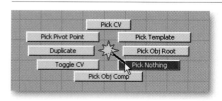

Maya is a selection-heavy package—much of its workflow is based on picking this or selecting that. One command that was useful in its predecessor Alias PowerAnimator was Pick Nothing, which deselected whatever was active. Sure, you can click on open space to do that, but often this bit of MEL is useful when used as a hotkey or especially when used for a custom Marking Menu, like in the next Killer Tip. Here is the command: `selectMode -root; select -clear.`

PREFS IN YOUR POCKET

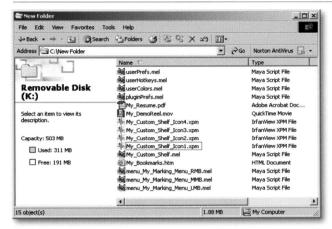

A handy habit of some Maya artists (facilitated by the advent of pocket USB drives) is storing all the customization you have worked long and hard to set up as a series of Maya pref files, found in the Maya\5.0\prefs folder in the Documents and Settings folder of your login directory. These MEL scripts contain all the work you have done with custom colors, Marking Menus, shelves, Hotkeys, and the like. Simply copy these into your new workstation's pref folder, and you are right at home. Also, some artists will carry a resume and current demo reel on the USB drive as well, which is very handy for the "migrant film worker" moving from shop to shop.

   ## WORKING YOUR UNITS

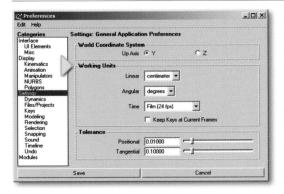

Maya began a previous life as Alias, an industrial design tool. Because Alias was a Canadian company, the metric system was used to describe geometry (a side note, Z is also commonly called "Zed" there, another joint Seussian/Canadian term). Because most industrial design products are smaller than a house and larger than a breadbox, centimeters were chosen as the default grid unit. Larger units can be specified, however, in Preferences, Preferences, Settings, Working Units. Most Maya artists believe it wise not to change these into Imperial units though because basic system calculations such as dynamics, lighting decays, and the like can be altered by doing so. So, if you need to work in feet and inches, consider 1 grid unit to be 1 foot and use decimal conversion of inches for input.

Y-UP VERSUS Z-UP

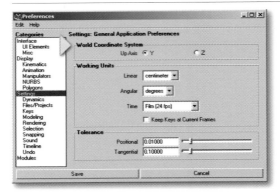

No, this is not referring to characters from a Dr. Seuss story, but rather the different coordinate systems Maya artists choose to work in. Architects and industrial designers commonly work in Z-up, as CAD systems often default to this system. Film and effects work is almost always done in Y-up, to complicate matters. One simple explanation for the two preferences is that architects and designers tend to work on objects that sit flat on a horizontal plane (thus the notion of depth, or Z runs up); whereas film makers work in a vertical plane (where the notion of depth or Z moves away from the camera). Maya can be set to operate natively for either one in Window, Settings/Preferences, Preferences, Settings, World Coordinate System. If you want to convert a model from Z-up to Y-up, simply group the model, rotate –90 in X, and then Edit, Ungroup, with the Preserve Position option checked.

   ### SMOOTH MOVER

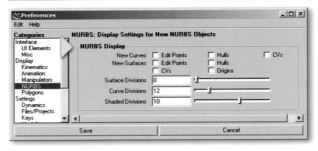

Maya's interactive graphic response is considered one of the fastest of 3D apps, and this is for a few reasons. The Open GL implementation is certainly very robust, but a lot of the speed is attributable to default coarse settings on line curvature and hardware shading samples.

That is generally a good thing, but if you do a lot of precision curve work or find yourself constantly setting NURBS shaded resolution higher than the keyboard stock 3 under Attribute Editor, NURBS Surface Display, Crv Precision Shaded, you can set it globally as a preference, found in Preferences, Preferences, Display, NURBS, NURBS Display. Set Curve Divisions to perhaps 12 and Shaded Divisions to 10. Now Maya will create beautiful looking objects out of the gate, giving you a luxurious look until you feel a need to place less burden on your graphics card and restore the defaults.

CLICK BOX SIZE FOR HIGH-RES MONITORS

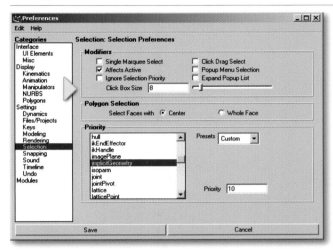

Sometimes selecting objects gets troublesome with curves or thin geometry, especially if you are used to running higher resolutions on your monitor. There is a remedy for this—go to Window, Settings/Preferences, Preferences, Settings, Selection Modifiers and increase Click Box Size from 4 to a higher number of pixels. Set it too large, though, and you will make selections too gingerly, so find the right area for your resolution.

TOP-PRIORITY CLEARANCE

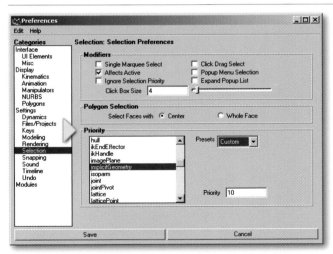

Maya has a dirty secret—it gives preferential treatment to NURBS over polys when selecting overlapping objects. Shocking, I know, but you can actually choose which gets picked first under Window, Settings/Preferences, Preferences, Settings, Selection, Priority. Just pick an entity type, choose Custom Preset, and raise or lower the priority to your liking. Equal rights for Implicit Geometry!

 ## WE DON'T NEED NO STINKIN' DYNAMICS

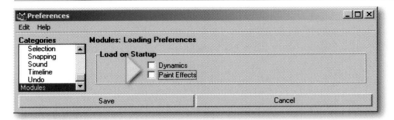

Another little secret is that two modules in Maya consume an inordinate amount of system resources—Dynamics and Paint Effects.

If Maya starts struggling because of limited RAM, consider turning off these modules, not in the Plug-ins Window as you might expect, but in Window, Settings/Preferences, Preferences, Modules, Load on Startup. If Dynamics or Paint Effects are needed in a scene, or if a command is invoked, they will load, but otherwise Maya will maximize the precious resources you have.

 ## DON'T LOWER YOURSELF TO COMPONENT MODE

Maya is set up to make CV selection in Component mode by default. A crafty bit of MEL can help display these Component level items while in Object mode, thus speeding up your workflow. Type this MEL and make a shelf item, or better yet, a Marking Menu item: `toggle -controlVertex -hull -editpoint;`. You can label it Toggle CV, and you might find it very useful with this Pick CV MEL: `selectMode -component; selectType -allComponents false; selectType -controlVertex true;`. Now all CV manipulation can be done without resorting to the lowly depths of Component mode.

```
// This is the Toggle CV cmd

toggle -controlVertex -hull -editPoint;

//This is the Pick CV cmd

selectMode -component;
selectType -allComponents false; selectType -controlVertex true;
```

MORE AND MORE IMAGE FORMATS

When rendering, Maya provides a basic, if somewhat peculiar, set of presets for resolution and formats in the Render Globals. Sometimes a production team will define a standard for proxy and final renders not found here, so here is little trick to avoid redundant typing when rendering repeatedly. Copy *Maya_Install_Location*\scripts\others\imageFormats.mel into your standard user Maya scripts directory. Then edit this file and add whatever formats you desire. Maya will always read from the users scripts directory first, but just make sure never to overwrite the original install directory scripts, which is generally a BAD thing.

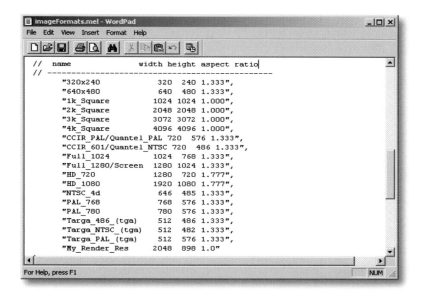

The Glamorous World of Modeling

Ah, the glamorous world of modeling. No, not the high-fashion supermodel kind, but rather the more sundry task of efficiently building our base surfaces.

The Glamorous World of Modeling

work smarter, not harder

Luckily for us, Maya is much smarter than your common supermodel. The modeling component in Maya owes its heritage to Alias, which was long considered the industry's pre-eminent NURBS modeler. Because of this, Maya's initial support was stronger for NURBS and lighter on polygonal modeling, but it is now very robust for both methods. Thus, here you will find a mixture of useful tips for both sides of the fence. Just remember that modeling is one area of CG production that, if not approached sensibly and lightly, can lead a team into a world of hurt, making the entire project painful rather than pleasant. So, let's hit the modeling runway—you look FABULOUS!

ALIGNED IMAGE PLANES

Because we frequently use three-view source imagery as a starting point for tracing or guiding our work, a useful technique is to use multiple image planes, each reflecting side, top, or front views, respectively. The trick is to align them properly so that we end up with Michelangelo's David instead of your sedentary Uncle Harry. Use View, Image Plane, Image Plane Attributes, Center values to shift the placement of each image plane so that they align with each other. Make sure your original Photoshop images have the same relative scale, or you might end up with your Aunt Edna instead.

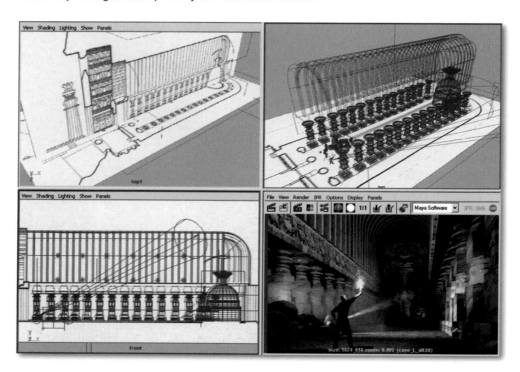

ALPHA ONION SKINS

A variation of the last tip is to map a reference image onto a NURB or poly card instead of using image planes. If the reference image is a drawing or is linework-based, copy the Color channel into the alpha in Photoshop, invert it, save it as a .tif, and then map it with a File Texture to the Color channel in a basic Lambert shader. The alpha will be respected when textured shading is used, turning the card into a transparent onion skin of linework. Next, turn down the Alpha Gain in the File texture node to fade it into the background and align as in the previous tip. Now place them into a layer and use Reference display mode to avoid selecting them during your modeling. They basically become 3D overhead transparencies— a bit more interesting than your garden-variety bar chart, however.

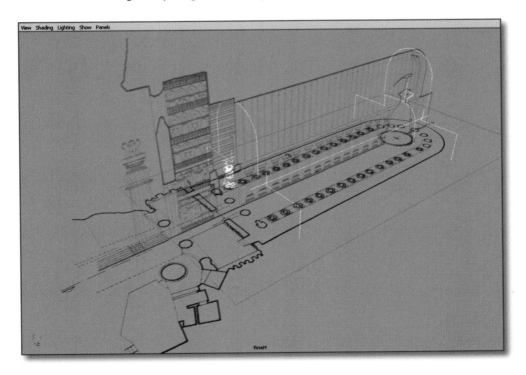

   ## MAYA CARD TRICKS

An excellent strategy for efficient rendering is to augment scenes with scanned images or animated texture maps onto flat surfaces, known commonly as cards or billboards. This is used to optimize an otherwise unmanageable scene or simply to add more detail cheaply. As an electronic version of paper dolls, there are limitations, because the elements must remain roughly perpendicular to the camera and in the background. Cameras cannot roam around them. A good application, though, would be crowd scenes, trees, cityscapes, or otherwise overly heavy background elements. Note that you must match the lighting in your card image to the scene in which they are being placed, possibly resetting some light direction in Photoshop using the Render Lighting filter. You must also mask out the object, making sure that the area outside the object's alpha is black. Now use this map in an Incandescent channel in a Lambert shader and turn the Color channel down to black. Map a file copy of the Alpha channel to the Transparency channel, which acts as a stencil and creates the look of complex geometry with the expense of a single polygon. Animated maps can be used as well, which are useful for tree leaf rustling or pedestrians walking. This very simple trick is used much more than you might think in many well-known film effects scenes. Just goes to show that the best tricks are often the simplest!

MAPPING VERSUS MODELING

One of the cardinal rules in efficient modeling is never model what you can map. Bump or Displacement mapping can replace surface detail and texture, and Transparency mapping can substitute for excessive repetition of simple elements, such as truss work or piping runs. Distant truss work or piping can be simulated reasonably well using the trick of adding a Bump map of a gradient created by path stroking an airbrush over a truss pattern in Photoshop. This effectively modulates the light normal into a tube-like highlight that otherwise would look flat and mapped.

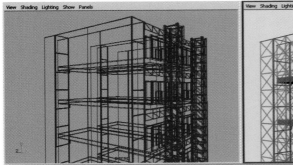

INSERT HERE WHILE DRAWING CURVES

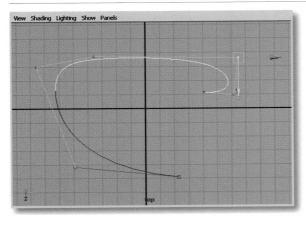

Here is a hot tip for modifying NURBS curves as you draw them. As you place CV points, hit Insert before finishing the command, and you will notice it gives you the transform jack to modify the current CV placement. Now press the up or down arrow, and it will move the jack to other points in succession. Hit Insert again and continue, or finish the curve. Pretty tricky, eh?

  EXPLICIT, R-RATED NURB TESSELLATION

Sorry, nothing too racy here, just a steamy hot tip that can dramatically speed your renders and reduce your modeling. Maya breaks a beautifully curvaceous NURBS surface into a polygonal mesh during the act of rendering, and it usually does a reasonable job of setting the amount of tessellation required. But as with all automatic things in Maya, it is best for you to decide what is proper. Pick a NURB surface, go to Attribute Editor, Tessellation, Advanced Tessellation, and enable it. If you check Display Render Tessellation in the Tessellation box above, you can compare what Maya is suggesting to a more optimal setting that you might make. Use Stick to Mode U, V of Per Span # of Isoparms, and raise and lower the Number setting until that chunky monkey becomes as smooth as a baby's behind. And you thought there was no nudity involved in this tip.

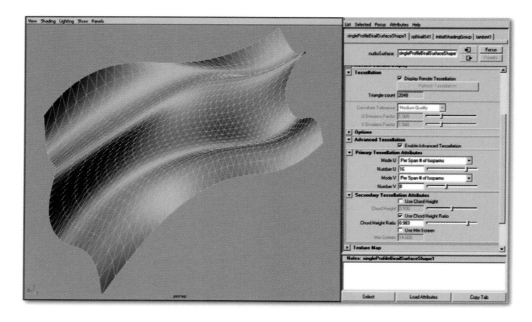

TESSELLATION VERSUS CVS

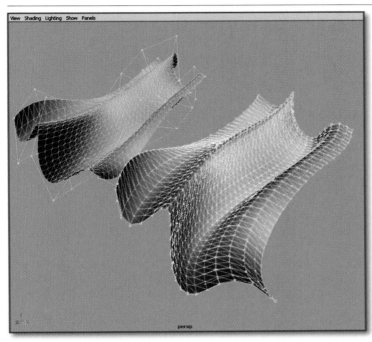

As we just covered in the previous tip, subdivisions are a necessary parameter to define adequate rounding of NURBS curved surfaces. Many fail to consider, though, that within modeling, the biggest factor affecting render times is subdivisions (tessellation settings) and how they are related to CV count. One can easily magnify the render time by multiple factors if subdivisions are not properly understood.

For instance, many surfaces have a flat component where a subdivision of 1 is all that is necessary. Remember that subdivision settings are relative to the span between isoparms, not the length of the surface. Therefore, if isoparms and the corresponding CV count are high, fewer subdivisions are needed. The inverse is true as well—if you have fewer CVs to describe an object (a good goal), then more subdivisions are required. You can see this is a push-pull relationship, and there are no magic numbers to define just how many CVs are necessary. Typically, it is best to rely on setting finer tessellation instead of adding CVs, which will build up the file size. The main point is to understand what your settings accomplish and optimize just to the point of noticeable faceting, as dictated by the proximity of the object. Setting manual subdivisions is a tedious affair, but if you integrate it into your workflow after each element is built and drink a pot of coffee at each sitting, it goes unnoticed.

LINEAR VERSUS CUBIC HEROICS

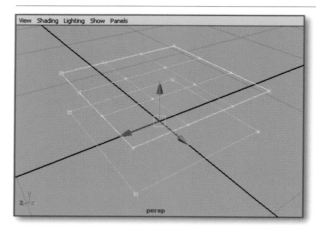

If you envy superhero antics and would like to get similar admiration and respect, try this tip. NURBS models can get notoriously unmanageable in size, often for no good reason at all. In the effort to reduce CV count, a major efficiency step is to use Degree 1 Linear modeling operations over Degree 3 Cubic for flats. The default and often-used setting of Degree 3 creates a minimum of 16 CVs in order to be able to deform a surface freely. Degree 1 restricts the CV count to 4 for a flat planar surface. If the surface never needs deformation and will remain planar (the bulk of architectural scenes or hard models, for example), model with the Degree 1 option. A many-fold savings will result in the weight of your model, creating room for further detail elsewhere. File size will be held down, RAM use will plummet, you will be hoisted up as a true hero, and world peace will ensue (we all hope).

   CONSTRAIN THOSE UNRULY CURVES

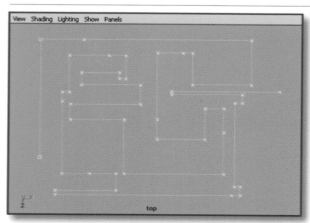

Here's a handy tip when drawing curves. Maya will constrain the next CV to horizontal or vertical axes with the simple addition of the Shift key. You may have known this since you were in diapers (it's been there since v1.0), but if not, it's a gem.

THE REVOLUTIONS WILL NOT BE TELEVISED

In our quest to eliminate unnecessary CVs, another very useful technique is reducing the number of sections in a revolve creation. You will notice that as the revolve sections are reduced, the circular profile becomes more oblong and distorted. For entertainment applications, accuracy is not a great factor, so this can be reduced from the default of 8 down to 4, 5, or 6. Also note that the distortion created will only be noticeable at the end profile, so for piping or tubing, it will appear indistinguishable from a higher section element. Again, this will vastly reduce CV count if the model has a fair number of revolves, such as a grimy boiler room containing huge amounts of pipework. Also, it helps to reduce midsection CVs on straight runs by lofting between two circles using the Degree 1 Linear option with 4, 5, or 6 CV circles (not the default 8).

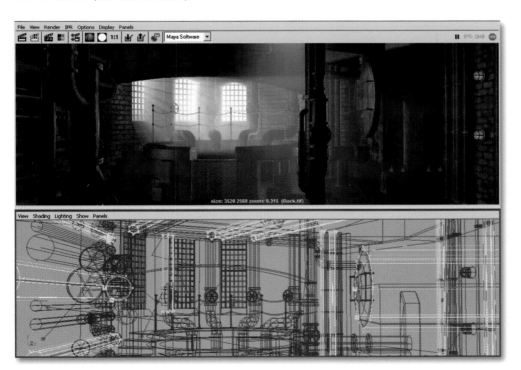

   BI-RAILING THE MISSING GLASS SLIPPER

If you ever find yourself needing to model a glass slipper for a CG feature animation involving fairy tales (it HAS happened), there is no better way than using the wondrous Birail command. This example is intended to show how Birail can solve some particularly sticky topologies, such as a shoe, by effectively sweeping a changing profile across two guide rails. If you can conceptually break forms down into this scenario, it can work wonders. In this case, draw shoe profiles in the top and side views. Now extrude or loft the side profile curves so that there is a horizontal extrusion that passes over the top profiles. Project a top profile curve onto the extrusion using Edit NURBS, Project Curve on Surface tool. Now pick that Curve on Surface and copy it using Edit Curves, Duplicate Surface Curves. Do the same for the lower profile and attach the side profile curves to the newly created rails. Use Surfaces, Birail, Birail2 Tool to create one half of the shoe. Now use Edit, Duplicate with a negative 1 in the X Scale filed to mirror the other side, giving you a shoe fit for a princess.

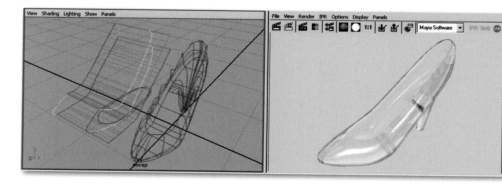

SLIPPER REBUILDING

One of the true great Swiss Army Knife commands in your modeling toolbox is Edit NURBS, Rebuild Surfaces. You can change U and V Degree, direction, and number of parameterization spans while retaining the boundary and shape of the surface. This comes in handy when optimizing surfaces or creating the right spans for animation behavior. Let's look at the shoe modeled in the previous tip. Let's say it is too heavy for a real-time game. Turn Spans to 1 and 1 and output to Polygon Quads. This is a NURBS command that often is more flexible to use than the NURBS To Polygons tool. Now let's say that we need to up-res the shoe for a close-up in an ad campaign. Turn Spans up to 20 and 20, output back to NURBS, and we have a gleaming glass slipper worthy of close inspection.

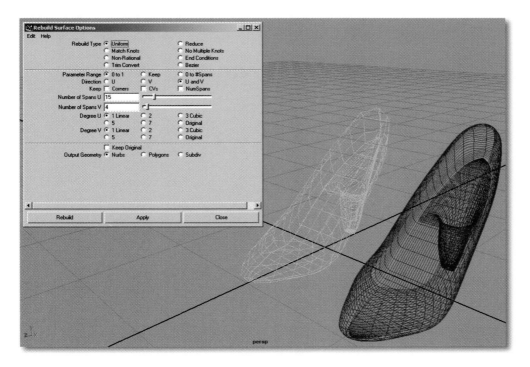

     SHADY, UNDESIRABLE ELEMENTS IN MAYA

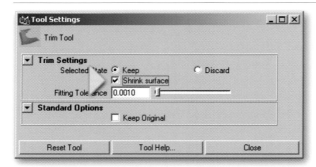

Maya sometimes provides tools that are initially attractive but end up creating problems in the production pipeline. An example is Trimmed Surfaces, an unavoidable and useful tool for creating odd shapes or holes in NURBS. Trims actually do not reduce ultimate geometry, though. Instead they offer what is in effect a masking of what is underneath. Alternatively, it is useful to create the trimmed surface, use Edit Curves, Duplicate Surface Curves to pull the profile curves, and then Loft or Birail derivative surfaces if possible. Another option is to use the Trim Tool option of Shrink surface. This will reduce the Trim to actual geometry instead of "hiding" it. Holes are a bit more of a problem, but they can be re-created by breaking the surface into discrete patches, or even by trying a transparency map instead. Another problematic command is Surfaces, Planar. A Planar face is a convenient way to create odd perimeters, but it suffers from the same Trim problems. Again, try a collection of patches with a projection map to make up for it, or better yet, use a polygonal surface for such shapes. Lastly, avoid using Edit, Duplicate with the Instance option on. Instances only reduce the working file size of the model, but when going out to render, they don't offer any savings. Therefore, a false sense of security can result as your file grows to unrenderable sizes, even though the file size might be tiny. Worse, Instance copies can create problems when grouping or ungrouping.

RANDOMIZE THOSE CVS

Here is a great trick for deforming objects without deformers. Say what? Actually, this is a
very easy way to slightly perturb surfaces without taking the time to tweak a deforming
operation. Simply take a NURBS or poly surface that you want to randomize, select all CVs or
vertices, and set a keyframe on them. Now open the Graph Editor and use a MEL randomizing script, such as RandKey.mel, found online at a site such as Highend3d.com. With the
script, randomize the value, not time, and update on the Time Slider. The surface will be
either too subtle or totally wrecked, so adjust accordingly. After adjusting it to your liking,
delete the animation on the surface because you will be carrying a lot of animation baggage you don't need.

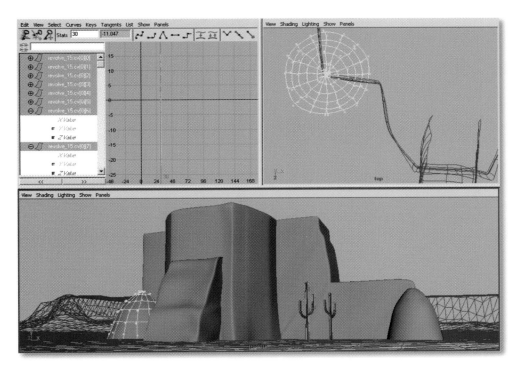

JUNKYARD DUMPING SIMULATION

Need to model a junkyard with piles upon piles of random objects, all resting on top of each other? You could painstakingly orient each one manually, or you could try this Killer Tip. Take the objects to be piled, raise them up in the air above a plane set at ground level, and with them all selected, choose Soft/Rigid Bodies, Create Active Rigid Body in the Dynamics menu set. With all of them still selected, select Choose Fields, Gravity. Now pick the ground plane and choose Soft/Rigid Bodies, Create Passive Rigid Body. Then play back until the pieces fall onto each other in a jumbled heap, saving you hours of tedious monotony. Aren't 3D apps great? Don't forget to lock down the objects and delete the extra dynamics baggage on the objects by choosing Edit, Delete by Type, Rigid Bodies.

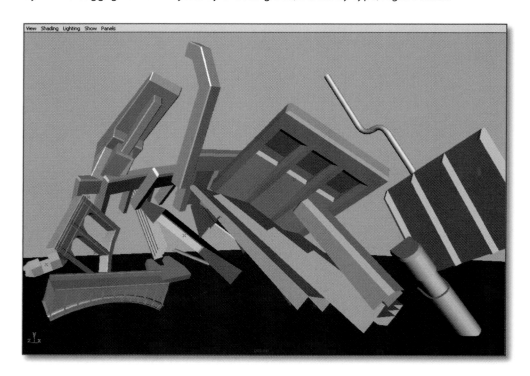

USE OF PHOTOSHOP AS A MODELING TOOL

Photoshop a 3D tool, you say? No, this is not a sneak preview of version 10.0. Instead it's an often-overlooked filter that's been available in Photoshop since version 1.0, found under Filters, Distort, Wave. Sometimes intricate design work needs to be generated for 3D modeling details, and this trick can speed up that process. First, start by drawing basic linework in Photoshop using marquees or lines. Then use the Wave filter with a very small number of Generators, perhaps one to two. Choose Square as the Wave shape, and select Repeat Edge Pixels. You should have a nice garbled and unusable image at this point. To make it shine, turn the Wavelength and Amplitude down very low and tweak as desired. When an aesthetically interesting pattern is formed, this can be autotraced as described in the following Killer Tip and implemented in your model as what the FX industry affectionately calls "Greeblies," or sundry tech details.

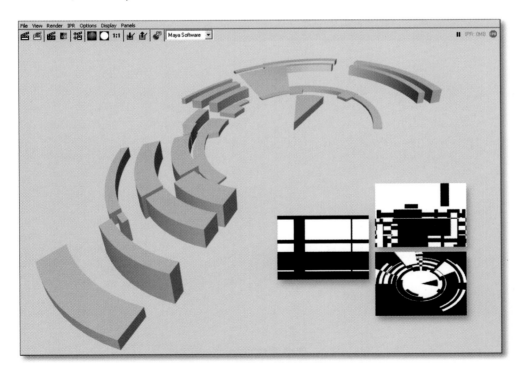

     AUTOTRACING FOR FUN AND PROFIT

Frequently, we are asked to do things we would rather not do, such as trace the entire shoreline of every continent on Earth. If you are paid by the hour, this might seem like a good deal, but another approach is to automate such menial tasks, which, if I remember correctly, is why computers were invented. Unfortunately, we do have to trace intricate artwork primitively on occasion with NURBS curves, so a rather nice alternative exists using a package designed primarily for graphic artists—Adobe Streamline. After scanned raster artwork is vectorized in this package, most graphics users will fail to see why DXF is provided as an output file type. 3D geeks will certainly see this as a GOOD thing in Martha's words, so at the push of a button, the work of a million monkeys is performed, and all the coastlines are yours in very fine detail (CV count) if desired. Remember that Maya DXF import in version 5.0 requires you to load the Dwg Translator plug-in from Window, Settings/Preferences, Plug-in Manager.

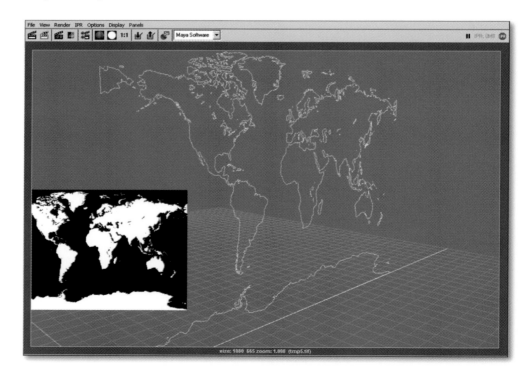

PHOTOSHOP PATHS TO MAYA CURVES

Here's a real magic trick for you Photoshop enthusiasts. Make a path in Photoshop, and then export it in Illustrator format. Now move over to Maya and recall that there was an Illustrator import option. Open the .ai file, and low and behold, it becomes a beautiful NURBS curve, with CVs placed wherever you put a path point in Photoshop. Now here's where it gets really good. Text in Photoshop has a Convert to Work Path command under the Layers menu, so any of the multitudes of fonts you have loaded in Photoshop become yours in Maya. Lastly, the autotracing that the previous Killer Tip pointed out with Adobe Streamline can effectively be done in Photoshop by using the Magic Wand or Color Range tool, converting into a Work Path, and sending the curves over to Maya for more fun and games.

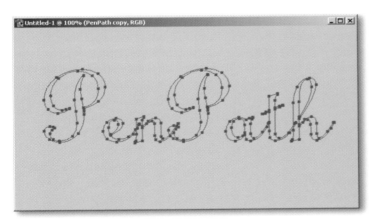

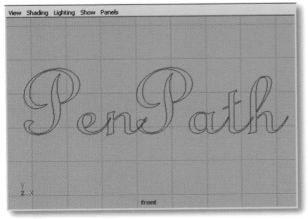

    WRESTLING WITH DISPLACEMENT

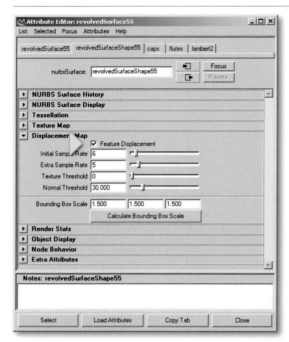

Displacements are one of the truly great, as well as truly painful, features in 3D. They are a magic bullet for creating detailed modeling that otherwise would be prohibitive or wildly heavy. But there is no free ride in life or CG, and displacements are a good example. Challenges arise when you try to get the exact resolution without artifacts, minimize RAM, and preview to facilitate camera animation. Maya has added Feature Displacement as the default method for tessellating the surface intelligently so that triangles are created only where they need to be. The problem arises from artifacts unique to this method, so you should first adjust Initial Sample Rate to capture the detail required, then start Extra Sample Rate at 0 and inch upwards to eliminate noise but retain detail. This differs from the older method of setting explicit NURBS tessellation to achieve detail. Feature Displacement should also help to alleviate the high RAM loads from earlier methods. Finally, to preview results, you need to convert to polygons via Modify, Convert, Displacement to Polygons. The mesh that is created can be only used for previewing, and then it must be discarded or hidden for final renders. If the mesh comes in too large, turn off Feature Displacement in the object's Attribute Editor but check back on render time.

ANIMATE YOUR MODELING

Two animation commands can have great utility when modeling—Animated Snapshot and Animated Sweep. If these are new to you, you are in for a treat. Both are found in Animate in the animation menu set. Animated Snapshot creates a copy of an animated object at selected frames along its performance. This can be used for abstraction or modeling utility if the animation is set up for that purpose. Animation derived from Expressions or IK will not be respected, though, so use Edit, Keys, Bake Simulation first. Animated Sweep differs in that is uses curves only, but it has the strength of being able to construct a monolithic surface from the animation. It is conceptually an extrude based on an animated path. Both of these are processing-intensive, but performance can be improved by turning off Construction History.

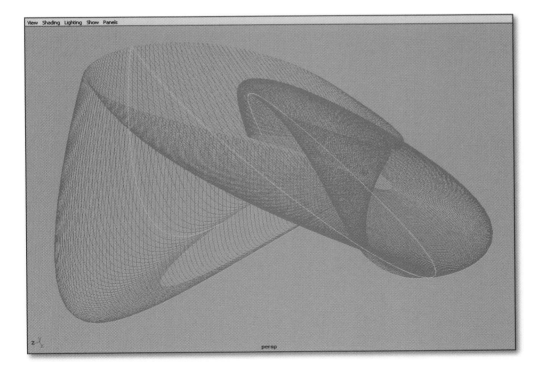

SET SUBTLETIES

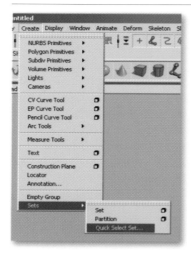

Grouping elements is typically useful for animation of those elements or for character work. For simple selection and hiding purposes, layers offer a nice GUI. But what if you need to preserve your carefully assembled selection of various objects, lights, and lattices without disturbing their existing grouping? Enter sets, a wonderful way of saving selections without the data overhead of groups or layers. Definition-wise, sets are useful for purposes beyond simple selection, partitions are for exclusive membership, and Quick Select Sets are the preferred type for general selecting. Make your selection and go to Create, Sets, Set/Partition/Quick Select Set. Enter a name, and then deselect the object. Do other work, and then go to Edit, Quick Select Sets, *your set name* to reselect that group without the tedium of carefully selecting a grouping again. Problem is, only you will know how clever you are.

TRANSFORM TOOLS SHORTCUT

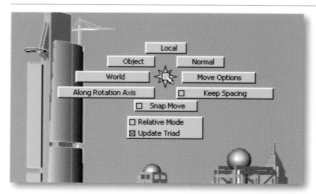

Here's a handy little gem when needing to push and pull points or objects around in different orientations. Select an object and hit the usual w, e, or r transform shortcuts, but in this case, keep it pressed, and press the left mouse button anywhere on screen. You are presented with the same options as when you double-click a transform command such as World, Object, or Local Space selection. Quite a timesaver when manipulating points.

INTERROGATING POINTS AS TO WHERE THEY LIVE

Finding the exact location of a pivot point or object center is trivial, but on occasion you might need to find the exact coordinate location of a CV or poly vertex. Make a point selection, open the Script Editor, and type this to call back the X,Y,Z coordinates:

```
xform -q -t -ws;.
```

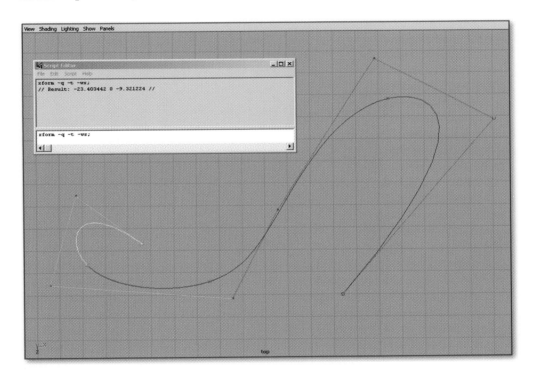

   FACE PROPOGATION VIA SHELL IN POLY SELECTION CONSTRAINTS

I had to use one tip title that sounded pretty technical, so here you are. This is actually a straightforward but powerful trick that can save a lot of hair roots. Pick a poly object, go into Face Component mode, and pick a face. If you now need to pick all connected faces, this can be a chore because of model complexity and/or overlapping UVs. The hot ticket here is to propagate face, vertex, or UV selection using Edit Polygons, Selection, Selection Constraints. When open, choose Shell Propagation and then select Close and Remember. Now pick a face, vertex, or UV, and every one related to that one will be picked automatically. This also comes in handy when trying to separate and manipulate groups of related UVs in the UV Texture Editor.

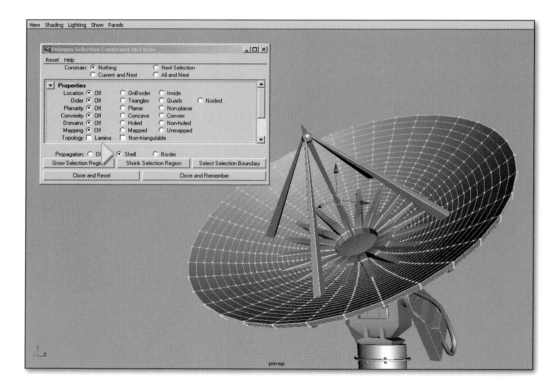

Embracing the Revolution

the

Revolution

Lighting Your Way

Lighting in Maya is, ironically enough, a "dark" art—there just aren't any cookbook recipes to follow. If you gave 100 Maya artists the same task to light a space or character, you would probably end

Embracing the Revolution
lighting your way

up with 100 different results. Of course on a big project this could pose a major problem, so teams spend time creating standard rigs and approaches, but in general lighting is more an intuitive art than a standardized craft. It is responsible for the success of a scene more than any other factor, but above all it is just plain difficult. Adding to that difficulty is the fact that of all CGI technologies, it has been the most difficult to create photorealism with lighting because of the crudeness of the tools available. However, a major revolution is underway—Global Illumination. GI offers a simulation-based approach to lighting that is light years ahead in terms of accuracy, though it sacrifices a bit of the carefully sculpted lighting of the artist. Whereas most 3D development is evolutionary, GI is revolutionary, and it is rewriting all our longstanding methods. We are currently in the middle of this revolution, so luckily older and well-proven approaches are still valid because the new ones are being put into serious production stresses. Therefore, you will find Killer Tips on both sides of the lighting movement in this chapter. Viva la revolucion!

TWEAKING LOTS O' LIGHTS

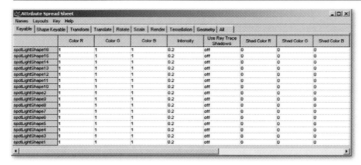

Undoubtedly you have created vast multitudes of lights (Maya artists LOVE lights) and had to globally change them for some reason or another. Rather than progressively altering them individually in the Attribute Editor, try the Attribute Spread Sheet. OK, maybe you have tried that, but what if you need to change all the more obscure attributes, such as Shadow Map Resolution? You may have found those attributes are missing. The trick is to use the down arrow key to select the Shape nodes and load all the previously hidden attributes under the All tab of the Attribute Spread Sheet.

REUSE THOSE DEPTH MAPS

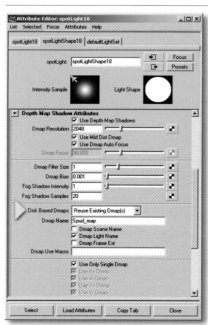

Maya has gotten very quick at calculating Shadow Maps, but over the course of thousands of frames, all that calculating can add up. If nothing moves substantially in your scene or background, consider Depth Map Shadow Attributes, Disk Based Dmaps, Reuse Existing Dmap(s) in the Attribute Editor of the light. This will write out the maps into *Your_project*\renderData\depth directory. They will not be deleted, as is the norm, and they will be reused for every frame. This can substantially cut down your renders if the shadow can stay still. For a character that moves, consider a linked light, which calculates on every frame. Lastly, remember that these depth maps can be inspected with Fcheck and the "z" key, which is very handy when trying to debug shadows.

COOKIES AND GOBOS

Sounding like something yummy from your childhood, these are rather old Hollywood terms for ways of manipulating the spread of light. Cookies and Gobos are actually paddles or cards with random holes cut out to deflect key lights into a draping of light and shadow or to soften the spread. Defining the signature look of the Film Noir period, they are useful for dramatic effects or simply for richening up a scene. Cardinal Rule #1 in CGI is that *Imperfection Is Your Goal*, so here is a great way to emulate that technique using a simple CGI spot light. First, paint a few random black and white organic patterns in Photoshop and save out as a .tiff file. Now create a Spotlight in Maya, and in the Attribute Editor, map a File Texture to the Color channel. Choose a Gobo file of your choice and adjust Filter Offset in the Spotlight Attribute Editor to add blur and softening to the sharp contrast. Adding warm hue into the Texture File Color Gain and cool hue to Color Offset can create further interesting effects.

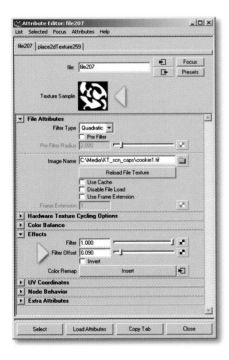

without gobo

with gobo

LIGHTING WITH PAINT

Allen Daviau is one of Hollywood's top Directors of Photography. An interesting statement he once made is that he often not only "paints with light" as the saying goes, but rather "lights with paint," using stage painters to attenuate surfaces into proper exposure. Conceptually, we do the same thing with our shaders. Lighting is inseparably intertwined with our surface properties. One shader attribute that has great usefulness to lighting is Incandescence Mapping. This is a terrific method to add or replace the appearance of lights. It is limited though because it doesn't offer a lighting solution for objects per se but is simply an illusion or painting of light appearing in the scene. The Incandescence attribute channel of a shader simply takes the color map and renders it at full (or at a potentially partial) value. The trick here is to use a painting program such as Photoshop to pre-paint the lighting onto a simple render or screen grab of the surface. In Photoshop, the Render Lighting filter is very useful here; just keep the Ambient slider set to zero in that plug-in. For architectural scenes, it is a great way to simulate the appearance of hundreds of lights without even containing a single one, as the almost entirely incandescent mapped example shows.

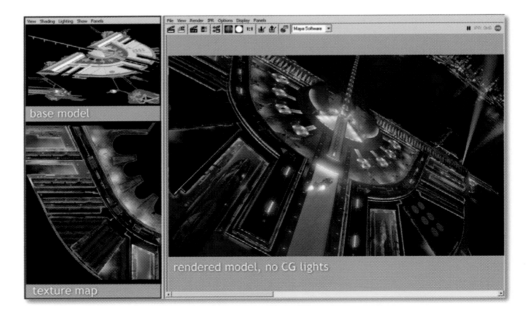

KILL THAT AMBIENT!

I don't normally condone violence, but there is really no place for ambient lights in good CGI. A better solution is to create a Directional light cluster by copying a handful of six or so Directional lights and placing them into a grouped cluster around a single pivot. Now rotate them counter to your main key and begin to rotate them apart, effectively giving light from multiple directions but enabling etching of sculpted form to occur, which a stock Ambient light naturally kills. The trick of course is to keep intensities down enough to not notice their directional sourcing. One option is to turn off the Emit Specular component in the light Attribute Editor.

  CUBIC POINT ARRAYS

Another great way to avoid the evils of Ambient Lights is to use an array of cubic decay Point lights. In the case of lighting an interior space, Ambient Light will unify everything into a monotonous flattening. A collection of Spot lights can accentuate certain forms but doesn't really offer a way to do an overall space. Area lights are best for this task, but they can drastically increase render times. A good compromise that offers more flexibility and a GI look is to fill the space with overlapping spheres of quickly decaying light provided by Point sources. Effectively a manual setup of an Area light that is tailored to the space, this method almost always provides a good solution for roughing out an interior scheme. Begin by placing an array of Point sources vertically midway from the ceiling to floor and spaced at that same distance apart. You may end up with rows of lights to fill the room, perhaps up to 20 or 30 lights. Adjust the intensity to equal a net level of 1.0, that is, 10 lights at intensity 0.1 for each. The key here is to use the highest rate of decay—Cubic. The intensities will run very high (about 2000), but it is abstract. With the fast falloff, pockets of shadow will accumulate in the corners, mimicking a GI render with a fraction of the render time. Additional Spot lights can be added for warm or cool shifts and accents on interior elements. A weak Directional light can be used to pull forward any wall that may need accenting over others. Note we have used no Ambient lights in this strategy. Lastly, don't turn on Shadow Maps on these Point lights, which is explained in the next Killer Tip!

FEAR OF POINT LIGHT SHADOW MAPS

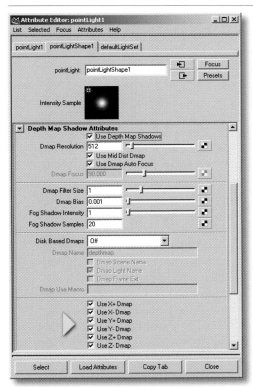

One thing that many artists overlook is that using Shadow Maps on a Point light does not generate one map, but six! As Shadow Maps are effectively renderings taken from a point in space to cover a 360-degree area, Maya adds six hidden spot cones, rotated 90 degrees to each other about the Point light center. Each cone angle's coverage is 90 degrees and is square, providing a full surround. Maya is considerate enough, however, to provide a way to turn off these maps under Depth Map Shadow Attributes, with check boxes for Use XYZ+– Dmap. Not that you can't theoretically run 120 shadow maps on 20 lights on a render (though it's probably not a good idea), but now you will know why your box sits there for hours, lost in thought before even rendering a pixel.

    LIGHT COLOR MAPPING VERSATILITY

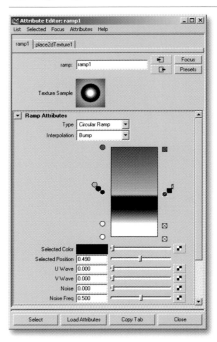

A valuable aspect of Maya lights is the capability to map the Color channel in the Attribute Editor. This simply places an orthographic section cut of your Spot light's color pixels with a rectangular or solid map of your choice, and it offers potential for many varied effects. First, it is useful for custom-designed penumbras. Apply a 2d Ramp Texture node to the Color channel of the light and create a grayscale circular ramp. This acts as a secondary means of controlling the falloff of light within the penumbra already set by changing the effective light color out from the center. Another common use is to assign a 2d Fractal Texture node to the color but adjust for low contrast, so that the even light is randomized to a slight "blotching." If done subtly, this introduces a scale factor and rich irregularity to cast light. The next obvious use of this is to connect a 2d File Texture node, acting as a slide projector of sorts. Lastly, the look of multiple lights can be simulated with one light by mapping a 2d Grid or Bulge Texture or a repeated circular ramp to give the appearance of a light passing through a diffuser. If Shadow Mapping is turned on together with Light Fog, multiple beams will be defined, giving you an instant disco!

POOR MAN'S GLOBAL ILLUMINATION

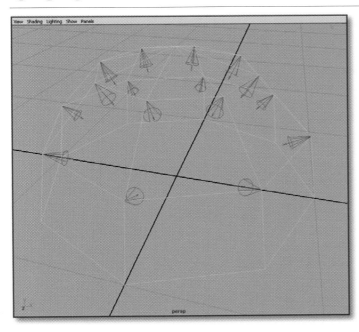

In the constant quest to achieve the look of Global Illumination without the associated exorbitant render costs, many have adopted the use of hemispherical layouts of traditional Spot or Directional lights. Web sites such as Highend3d.com have some excellent rigs available for download, such as GI Joe. If you feel ambitious enough to make your own, create a poly sphere with Subdivision Axis of 8 and Subdivisions Height of 6. Delete the lower faces to leave a dome. Create a Spot light, scale to .1, and then snap to one of the vertices. Turn on the Manipulator Tool in the Toolbox and grid snap the focus point to 0,0,0. Copy the light to the next highest vertex and reposition its focus back to 0,0,0. Center each light's pivot back to 0,0,0 and use Edit, Duplicate to copy the two Spot lights 7 times with a 45-degree Y rotation. Group the Spot lights, delete the sphere, and turn on Shadow Mapping with 1024 Map Resolution. Now export the dome as active and import into a scene. Scale up the top node of the lights while choosing Panels, Looking Through Selected on a single Spot light to maximize the area covered by the Shadow Map. Render away, and you get a poor man's version of GI shading. For a middle-income version, try GI Joe, where an environment map can inform each light's color for an HDR fake, and the number of lights used is far higher for smoother shadowing. For an upper-crust earner, try true GI and HDR rendering in Mental Ray. Expect to pay for the privilege, though.

HDR GI CGI TLA

High Dynamic Range is more than another of those geeky TLAs (three-letter acronyms); it is a fantastic way to match CGI into photographic backgrounds using photography itself to act as the only lighting source. At its highest implementation, it relies on Global Illumination raytracing to provide all lighting and shadow into the scene, albeit at a costly rendering expense. HDR can be faked somewhat using GI Joe, mentioned in the previous Killer Tip, but now that Mental Ray is native in Maya, the doors are wide open. To start, acquire a HDR file online, such as those found at Debevec.org. Make sure it is in latitude/longitude format, as opposed to spherical. Open Window, Settings/Preferences, Plug-in Manager to check to see if Mayatomr.mll is loaded. Create a sphere and scale it up well past the scene you have created. Now create a Lambert shader, and assign the HDR image to a File Texture mapped to both the Color and Ambient color channels. Make sure your scene objects have Blinn or Phong shading models, as you need reflectivity attributes. Add a light of any type, but turn its intensity down to zero—this will prevent Maya from using its default lighting. Render using Mental Ray, and turn on Final Gathering. Often, HDR rendering is too dark or light at the outset, so use the Color Gain value of the HDR File Texture to adjust, using values above 1.0 if necessary. Use Draft quality to check results, then try Production quality around the time to take a dinner break.

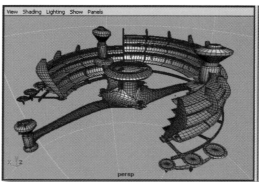 

PAINT THOSE SHADOWS

After all that previous discussion on snooty high-brow rendering technique, let's dumb it down (in a good way). Shadows can actually be cheated in a very easy and successful way by painting them in. There are various ways to accomplish this, from painting them into textures to creating shadow planes under objects. Let's look at a great way to add them where you need them using Layered Shaders. In this illustration, soft shadows were required for the beams overhead in this Native American kiva. Rather than use expensive GI, a Layered Shader was constructed with layers of soft shadow images created in Photoshop. Started by screen capturing the top view of the elements, it was pen path stroked by an airbrush in Photoshop into a clean layer and saved out as a .tiff file. The Layered Shader in Maya effectively composites the multiple layers, and it can mix shading modes like Lambert and Blinn onto the same surface. Use of Lambert for the shadow layers ensures the lack of unrealistic specular washes in the shadowed areas. Shadows on the walls are added by applying a 2d Ramp Texture to the Color Gain of the 2d Texture File, multiplying it down toward the ceiling. Lastly, the woven bowl and structures on the floor have shadow plates below them, to be discussed in the next tip.

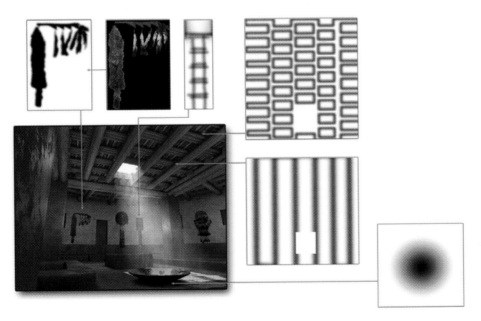

SHADOW PLATTERS

Pronounced Shadow "Plaa-tairs" in French, this highly advanced tip will challenge even the most astute PHD (another TLA). Ok, here we go, try to follow: Create a NURBS or poly plane, position it just above the floor surface and below your shadowing object, and attach a Lambert shader. Make the color black and map a 2d Ramp texture to the Transparency channel. Make the ramp circular or box, add a bit of Noise in Ramp Attributes, and render away. You are left with a beautiful soft shadow with virtually no render overhead. If your geometry is complex like this pile of boulders, render them from top view and use a blurred alpha channel instead of the 2d Ramp Texture. Remember to turn off Casts Shadows in the shadow plate's Render Stats in the Attribute Editor. Tough, huh?

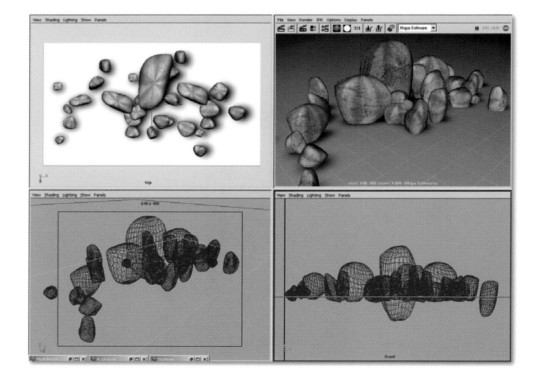

GLOWS, FOGS, AND FLARES, OH MY!

Maya lighting has the unique capability to simulate optical properties such as Glows, Fog, and Flares. These are quite useful in digital sets for their capability to simulate atmosphere and add presence to a scene. The use of fog to cast a visible spread of a spot, coupled with radial Flares or Glows onto the light, adds a great subtlety that contributes to the realism of the scene. Careful use of these effects is necessary, as they do have some pitfalls. First off, Fog effects are always preferable to Glows for a few reasons. Glows and Flares are a post-process render step, which can require large amounts of RAM and additional render times. If Fog effects are set up correctly, they can often match the look of more expensive Glow effects but result in fewer problems due to their true 3D world space description. Also, Glows can flicker on small objects annoyingly due to eye space auto-exposure calculation errors. A setup combination of dummy lights not casting light but contributing a Flare, Fog, and Glow component can add greatly to the scene. Often these can be pre-rendered and mapped onto a card using Incandescence Mapping. Or keyframe some animated 2d Fractal Noise into the Color attribute of the Fog, and a convincing atmosphere is guaranteed.

SHADOW MAP WOES

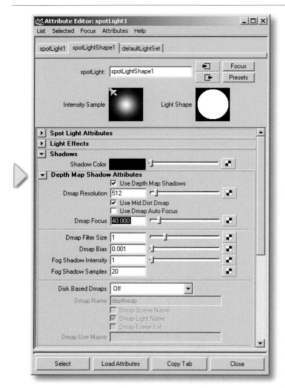

Shadow Maps (Dmaps) are a necessary evil in 3D. They are often fraught with instability and artifact issues, but their low impact on render times make them a necessary bedfellow. The default settings of a Spot light Dmap in Maya produce fast, soft, but not very accurate shadowing. To establish harder or more accurate shadow edges, it is necessary to adjust the parameters of Cone Angle, Dmap Resolution, and Dmap Filter Size. Typically start by narrowing the Cone Angle as small as possible, and then increase Dmap Resolution. If a softer look is required, try to increase the Dmap Filter Size, but beware of long render increases. Realize also that RAM use will rise dramatically with higher resolutions. For more accurate start points of the beginning of the shadow, or to reduce shadow artifacts, try a larger or smaller value of Dmap Bias. For greater stability in animations, always turn off Use Dmap Auto Focus and enter the cone angle value here. Often a certain combination is required with these settings, so render only on a selected few objects to test on and arrive at these settings quickly.

USE OF THRESHOLDED SHADER GLOWS

Shader Glow is a common effect added to a surface that aids the appearance of self-illumination, such as a glowing television screen or car headlight. It adds the appearance of the "blooming" of light due to high contrast or strong intensity. The problem arises as the entire surface equally glows by default, creating the look of an unfortunate nuclear accident on that to which you apply it. A little known control exists in the Shader Glow global attributes, found as an extra shader ball in the Multilister or Hypershade. Locate Threshold in the Common Shader Glow Attributes, and you will find that as it is raised, only the specular highlights will then bound the apparent glow effect. The end benefits of this technique are to show a light blooming effect in your renders and impress others at cocktail parties.

DANCING FIRE LIGHT

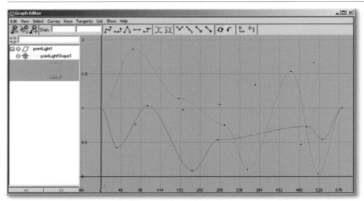

Here is great simple trick for animated light from a campfire or candlelight. Place a Point light in the center of your flame and keyframe a rich saturated color for the starting frame. Advance to the end frame and set a key. Now open the Graph Editor and add multiple keys across time in all the RGB curves present. Locate a randomizer MEL script, such as RandKey.mel found at Highend3d.com, and use it to randomize all the intermediate keys you just created. Now, because the keys on each of the curves are diverging from each other on the R, G, and B channels, the lighting will change color temperature and intensity during playback, giving an eerie life to the fire that you have rendered.

   LINK THOSE LIGHTS

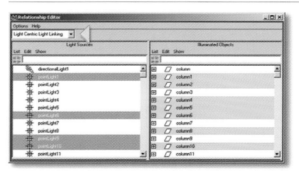

A useful technique to use for greater efficiency or just to get you out of tight places is light linking. Light linking enables a surface to be solely lit by a particular light, effectively pulling it out of the scene. This should be used judiciously, as the scene can quickly look unnatural. At times, though, it is useful for setting up a lighting that cannot occur with standard CG direct illumination lighting, such as light transport phenomena of bouncing or washing around objects. To use light linking, select the surfaces and lights desired and choose Lighting/Shading, Make Light Links from the Rendering menu set. Selecting Window, Relationship Editor, Light Linking gives you the ability to inspect connections and choose Light Centric or Object Centric, enabling flexibility in which is attached to which.

SHADOW LIGHTS

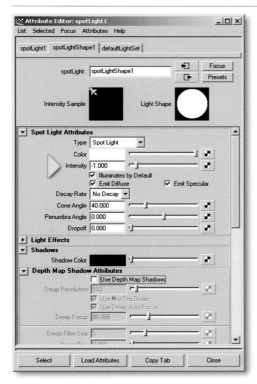

Possibly one of the most useful lighting techniques I use, Shadow lights are indispensable once you get used to them. They effectively enable you to place shadows independently of your lighting, something that a more flexible renderer such as RenderMan excels at. They also are very easy to set up and use. Start by creating a Directional light to provide the general key lighting. Next, create a Spot light of Intensity 1 and turn on Shadow Mapping. Adjust the Cone Angle and Penumbra Angle as you might want it for shadow purposes. Duplicate this light in the same position, but turn off Shadow Mapping and put −1 for intensity. The light components cancel each other out, leaving only the shadow. Group the two together and throw shadows exactly where you want them at any resolution. This is an excellent tip for large scenes where the Shadow Map gets too diffuse for the scale involved. Lastly, try Matt Wood's MWShadowLight.mel from Highend3d.com; he has made it plug and play by writing expressions between the key Attributes of the two lights. Shadow on!

LIGHT CYCLES

No, this is not a reference to Tron (that is if you are one of the three people who saw it) but rather a cool feature of Spot lights that may have slipped past you. Select a Spot light and hit the Show Manipulator Tool below the Scale button on the Toolbar, or better yet just hit "t." You are presented with the focus and pivot locators for the light, which is handy in itself, but you may have not noticed the tiny clock icon to the side. It is the Light Cycling Index, a fancy name for a button that cycles through different interactive adjustments for the light, from cone and penumbra width to decay regions. Now use Look Through Selected on the light and notice that is has added interactive barn door edges, making that task very speedy when lighting your homage to Tron.

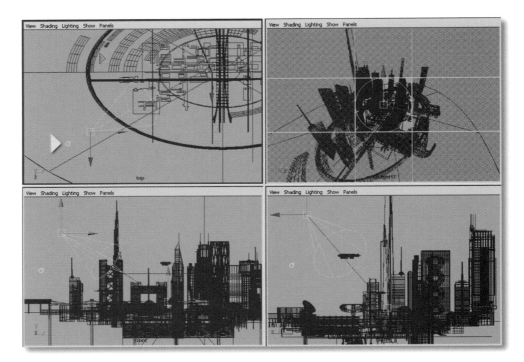

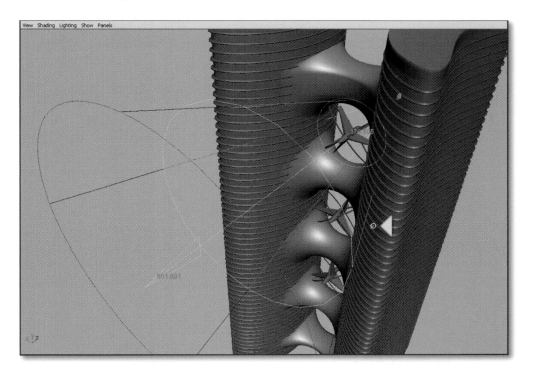

SPOTLIGHT DECAY REGIONS

Spotlight Decay Regions are handy when you need well-defined foggy searchlights to light from lampshades. Use the Light Cycling Index mentioned in the previous Killer Tip to display an interactive series of rings that define the borders of where light will occur. Adjust them so that the light begins outboard of the origin of the cone so that light and fog are not revealed until appropriate.

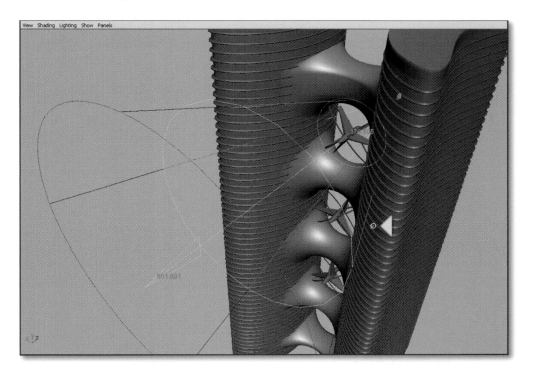

    CONSULTING SUN CHARTS

In film work, we are constantly combining CGI with photographic backgrounds or "plates." Matching up the lighting so that it is seamless is the real work. It all starts by determining where the sources were during the shoot. On a stage, this can be found by analyzing all of the measurements and survey data usually recorded. But what if the shoot took place outdoors, with the sun as the primary available light source? Some packages have coded in the ability to enter time of day, year, and location to recreate the sun vector direction, but Maya has not added that feature yet. In the meantime, use what architects use to determine solar angles—a sun chart. These can be found online or in solar energy guidebooks. Follow the time of day and year to locate the associated bearing and azimuth angles, and then use those to set the rotation of your key light. Shadows and highlights should now play well with each other. This is an inevitable MEL script to be written—any takers?

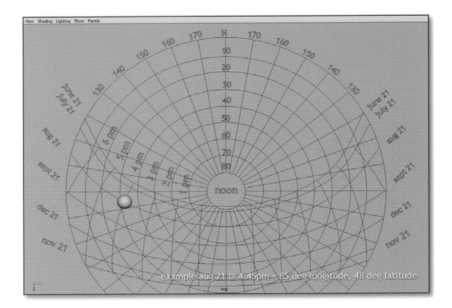

DIRECTIONAL SHADOW MAPS

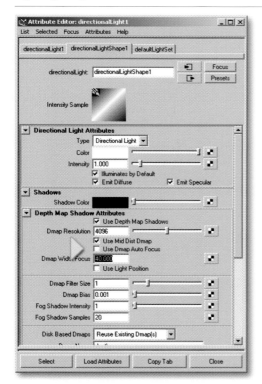

The use of Shadow Maps with Directional lights poses a problem. They look good, as the shadows look more uniform and parallel, but it is often very hard to get decent resolution. It is not hard to see why if you realize that the spread of the map is applied based on the largest object in your scene. It you are rendering a still life of a bowl of fruit, that is fine, but if you are rendering the island of Manhattan, one shadow pixel may spread across a street. Luckily, Maya gives us an option to apply a reduced cone angle to the spread, Use Dmap Auto Focus. Uncheck it and key in a smaller number, based in degrees from the centerline of the directional. The Directional light now begins to act like a Spot light, so position matters for proper application of shadows. The Use Light Position switch uses the location of the light to determine if objects behind or in front are considered in the shadow map. If lack of resolution still poses a problem, consider using the Shadow light technique described in a previous Killer Tip in this chapter instead.

Rags to Rendering

No Bad Rendering Any Time

At the end of the day, it all comes down to the rendering. Character performance carries the emotion, but rendering carries the eye. As with lighting, it is an

Rags to Rendering

getting a grip on shading

area in Maya where the talent and personality of the artist can shine through. However, many artists overlook the tremendous creative opportunities that Maya offers, relying on simplistic or downloaded shaders rather than understanding the true nature of building creative shader networks. Aside from being one of the better modeling packages on the market, Maya boasts one of the best creative environments for creating materials and shaders. Other renderers may be faster or less RAM-intensive, but the capability to quickly sculpt out a rich intended finish is a real strength of Maya. The node-based architecture inherent in the package carries over well into the shading environment, offering a rich array of connections and possible animated techniques. The recent addition of the Mental Ray renderer into the package further opens up the GI horizon for Maya artists. These rendering tips are gleaned from years of experience and will help you move from that flat shaded K-car of a rendering to a gleaming Lamborghini.

   IMPERFECTION IS YOUR GOAL

Not a motto from some 12-step rehab program, rather this is a good way to consistently approach texturing and shading. Good CGI is imperfect CGI because the eye is very sensitive to repetition and consistency. Basic ways to provide inconsistencies are slightly randomizing modeling vertices (as discussed in Chapter 3, "The Glamorous World of Modeling: Work Smarter, Not Harder"); mapping fractal texturing to lighting (as discussed in the previous chapter Chapter 4, "Embracing the Revolution: Lighting Your Way"); creating variations and grime in the texture map during painting; adding subtle random keyframes in your camera animation; and adding rich variations in the shaders themselves, such as randomness in specular, diffuse, displacement, and bump maps. The following image shows these principles applied. Every decision you make in the pipeline should be guided by this quest to be imperfect!

PROCEDURAL MAPPING VERSUS SCANNED FILES

The shading environment in Maya is very rich, and most of that depth is accessed from the tools offered under the Create Render Node menu initiated through the NASCAR flag button in a shader's Attribute Editor. A basic decision one must make under the Textures tab is whether to choose 2D or 3D textures. 2D textures generally are computed "slices of cheese," being either file textures from scanned imagery or procedural routines that only calculate a thin veneer of data. 3D textures are generally procedural solid "blocks of cheese," meaning that pure calculation is used to derive them instead of using predetermined texture maps to achieve a true volumetric representation. File textures generally consume few CPU cycles but lots of RAM, whereas procedural textures are the inverse. How you decide which to use depends on the nature of what you are trying to achieve, but if performance is a concern (when isn't it?), convert any calculation heavy 3D texture to a speedy 2D file texture using Multilister, Edit, Convert to File Texture. For those preferring the Hypershade, use Hypershade, Edit, Convert to File Texture. The original 3D shader is discarded and reattached to a new shader with the 2D file substituted. Ah, the joys of automation.

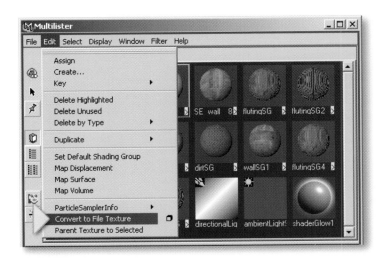

   MULTILISTER VERSUS HYPERSHADE—QUE ES MAS MACHO?

Maya always offers multiple ways to skin the cat, as the saying goes. One example is the interface options available to create shader networks. A holdover from the days of Alias PowerAnimator is the Multilister, a basic layout of shader, light, and camera nodes. In an effort to modernize, Maya has added the Hypershade panel to replace it, adding a snazzier name, more consolidation of tools, and a way to visually inspect connections between shader networks, not unlike the Hypergraph for geometry. Both accomplish the same end, so use the one appropriate to your preference or need. Functionally, the Hypershade has surpassed the Multilister, but the Multilister is preferred by the old guard because it's speedier and it provides a very direct way to inspect which nodes are connected to a particular network. The Hypershade is preferable for learning how connections are made, but it often tells more than is needed for basic connections. So, the Multilister is better for those who don't need the slowdown of graphic layouts of their networks, whereas the Hypershade is better for those who want to pick them apart or rearrange precise connections. Que es mas macho is up to you.

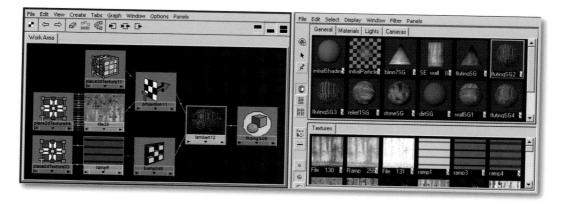

BAKING THE LIGHT

Though it sounds like an art film title, baking light is a handy way to speed up renders by converting lights into Incandescence maps. The downside of course is that there is no real lighting for characters to interact with, but for static background surfaces, it is a great optimizing method. However, remember that you are trading CPU cycles for RAM use as the light calculation becomes a map. To bake light, select the objects you want to bake onto, go to the Multilister and select the Shading Group assigned, and then go to Multilister, Edit, Convert to File Texture options. Check Bake Shading Group Lighting and Anti-Alias and choose an appropriate resolution. Note that shadows can also be baked in. Accept, and the geometry will be assigned to a new shader that has the lighting maps already attached. Note that it will create a Surface shader by default, so if more control is desired, create a new Blinn shader, connect these maps to the Incandescence channel, and turn Color to black.

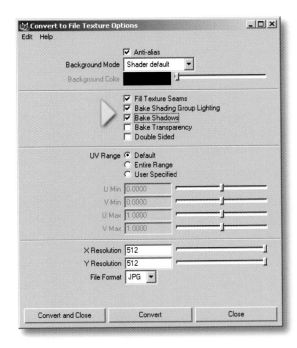

COLOR OFFSET AND GAIN—THE KEY TO SHADER NETWORKS

Maya shader networks really open up when the Map button is exploited to create chains of operations in order to reach an end result. For instance, instead of looking at the Map selections as an end target selection, look at it as the beginning of a range of possible connections. A typical use of "Map Chaining" is to use the Color Gain and Color Offset map buttons under most texture node's Color Balance section to chain ramps or files in order to shape or sculpt a desired look. Much more than a simplistic level adjustment, Color Gain is a multiplier, enabling multiplication of one file by another. This can modify or erode a texture file, enabling multiple multiplication events that can form very useful looks. For instance, areas can be cut away from an image because a black region (for example, 0,0,0) is multiplied by the source pixel value (for example, 1,1,1), creating a black region in that area. This can be driven from any 2D or 3D Texture, but frequently Ramp Textures are used. Likewise, Color Offset, which is mathematically an add function, enables an addition of texture to an existing file. Creativity can really open up when successive and clever connections are made with these two strategies. For example, a brick wall can be made by first multiplying a Grid Texture onto the Alpha Gain of a Fractal Texture Bump map. Next, 2D Noise Textures can be added to the Grid Texture connected through the Grid's Alpha Gain to disturb the precise grid linework. Alpha Gain and Offset are used over color operators because Bump mapping is an 8-bit process and uses these for its calculations. Thinking of all connections as effective math operations can enable end results to be better understood and predicted. Generally, though, Color Gain acts as a subtractive device due to its multiplication, and Color Offset acts as an additive device. Shaping or modifying textures can lead to really fantastic results (especially animated), and you will enjoy the use of this knowledge for some time to come.

THE JOY OF RAMPS

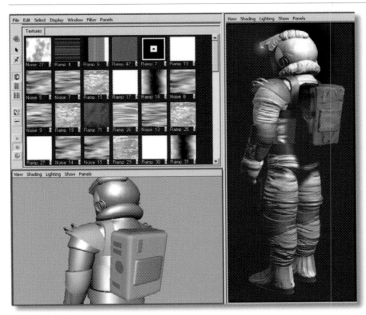

Another great tool in your rendering arsenal is the Ramp Texture. Used for much more than color blends, the Ramp Texture is the true workhorse of the shader creation workflow. By capitalizing on the Ramp Texture's UV options, noise functions, and Color Gain/Offset chaining capabilities, this seemingly simple tool can be put to clever use. Also, the capability to pipe a texture node into each slider makes the Ramp Texture very powerful indeed. Make sure you understand and explore the excellent noise function made available in the Ramp Texture. The noise in the general Ramp Attributes section is for spatial distribution, whereas the HSV Color Noise section can enable the creation of very subtle variations, which are a great way to introduce imperfections into many aspects of your work. Trying out the various Ramp Texture distributions found in the Type pull-down menu can provide a basic array of geometric forms. Another great trick is to pipe a texture through the Ramp Texture using Color Gain to add noise or imperfections. With ingenuity, texture maps can be replaced with simple Ramp Textures, as the spaceman example shows.

THE UNDERDOG OF SPECULAR MAPPING

Specularity is often overlooked as an important attribute in lieu of more developed color mapping or bumps. In fact, it is the key to true photorealism. A flat, consistent specular highlight rarely exists in the real world, so by perturbing your highlights with Specular mapping, you can get a more natural and convincing look to objects. It is also a key method for separating appearances of differing materials that have various specular behaviors. Study highlights on objects around you and think of how you might map the effects. With metals, adding color and variance to the specular look is essential. Start by using a 2D Fractal Texture mapped to the Specular Color on a Blinn shader. Next, change the UV repeats of the fractal down to 0.2 and 0.2 to create a broader wash, lower the Fractal Amplitude to reduce contrast, and then add a warm hue into the Color Gain and a cool hue into the Color Offset. This will create a color shift into the specular, giving a slight iridescence as the camera moves. With proper adjustment, your surfaces will become much more photorealistic and richer in behavior as the camera moves over them.

HEAVY METAL RENDERING

CG metallic surfaces can range from banal flying logos to lustrous beat up heat-distressed jet engines. Metals can be done poorly without some guidelines, but they are pretty easy to achieve with the proper setup. Start with a Blinn shading model, reduce Diffuse (essential to metal), reduce Specular Rolloff, increase Eccentricity, use a high-frequency (UV repeats of 1000) noise bump map (very small bump value), and add a fractal specular map with warm and cool Color Gain and Offset as described in the previous tip. Map the Color Offset with a noisy hue Ramp Texture to add heat-distressed iridescence. This solution works well for weathered and corroded metals. For shiny new aluminum or chrome, use a good reflection map. With a bit of noodling in IPR, you should start to feel the metal getting heavy right in front of you.

   ## GREEN SCREEN PLAYBLASTING

Playblast is the staple diet of judging animation in Maya. It provides a quick hardware capture of successive frames in order to evaluate your animation moves in real time. In most cases it works fine, but a problem exists if you ever need an alpha channel to do a slap comp over live action or composite separate pieces of a model together. Because Playblast does not offer any alpha, a simple workaround is to create your own green screen there by changing the background color to green in Window, Settings/Preferences, Colors. Then do a simple chroma key in your compositing package. Because there is no anti-aliasing typically in Playblast output, alpha can be cleanly and neatly extracted. Simple but useful.

EMBRACING DIRT AND GRIME

Dirt and grime are not only an unavoidable part of life (especially with kids), but they are actually *encouraged* in CG rendering. A common method is to dirty up your texture maps, but an easier and more spatially coherent method is to use 3D procedural methods in Maya's shader networks. Create a basic Lambert shader with a dark black color and then use a 3D Solid Fractal Texture as a transparency map. Use this shader as an overlay to any other base shader underlay in a Layered shader. Adjust the Ripples of the 3D Fractal Texture to 1.0, 0.1, 0.1 to get the proper vertical streaking and density. Use of a grayscale Ramp Texture on the Color Offset can taper it down to create drip marks. Age can be accelerated by using a subtle noisy hue Ramp Texture mapped to the Color Offset of the color map to discolor and slightly yellow the object. Color Remap can be used to further alter the original color spectrum. Erosion can be made on the bump map with a Color Remap as well, altering and intensifying the bump map. Rust and iridescent oil can be created by color mapping a noisy hue Ramp Texture on top of the rest using another layer in the shader. The beauty of using solid procedurals in all this is that they will not display UV mapping artifacts and will scale properly in distance. Who knew you would grow to love dirt this much?

TRIPLANAR PROJECTION TO THE RESCUE

Projection maps are the mainstay of environmental surfaces for a few reasons. First, wall surfaces need continuity with each other because brick coursings and trim lines need to match wall to wall. Projections offer a worldspace solution to this problem. The problem arises when one needs to map irregular walls, perhaps at odd angles to each other. We all know of the basic planar or cylindrical projection. Triplanar projection is one of a few lesser-known projection types Maya offers that is highly useful for architecture. Triplanar should not be confused with common box or cubic projection, which emanates all projections from the center outward on six planar faces. Triplanar is similar to planar, but it offers three axes of projection, one of which is chosen by the normal of the surface. As long as a surface face is within 45 degrees of a given projection face, it will pick up that respective face. Clearly, this is not a projection type for curving or organic models, but for orthographic architectural forms, it is the magic bullet because all walls can be mapped in one fell swoop with one shader. The examples shown of the boiler room and stone temple were done with nearly one shader, with no messy UVs to clean up!

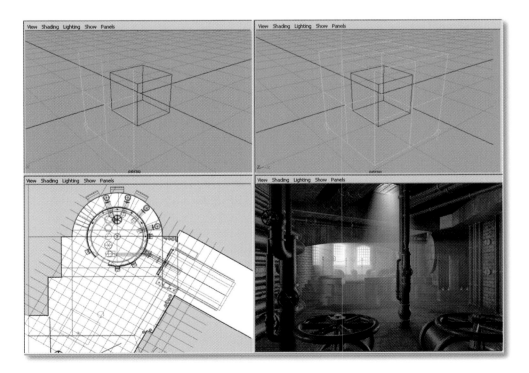

    LAYER IT ON

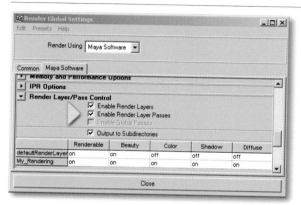

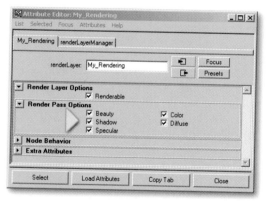

3D rendering is typically performed in one pass, which is known as rendering "in camera." For small projects or solo work, this is fine, but on large feature film projects where there are multiple chefs in the kitchen, this can be problematic. No one wants to re-render umpteen hours for a minute color change in your CG character's shoelaces. So rendering by layers or passes is commonly done, breaking one image into passes such as diffuse, specular, reflection, shadow, occlusion, HDR, z-depth, volumetric, matte, and so on, and combining them in a compositing package for fine control. This grouping may also be multiplied again by breaking elements up into foreground, midground, and background to enable easier matting or perhaps to handle an otherwise massive render load. Luckily, Maya has accommodated this workflow by establishing

Render Layers and Passes. Render Layers are created in the Layer Editor and used to isolate elements during a render. Render Passes are used to render the passes separately and can be found by highlighting a Render Layer in the Layer Editor and then choosing Layers, Layer Attributes. The Render Pass Options list the various choices. These can also be found in Render Globals, Maya Software, Render Layer/Pass Control by choosing Enable Render Layer or Passes. Note that you must Batch Render to enable any of this, and even though the Render Layer controls reside on the Maya Software panel, it controls Mental Ray output as well.

PASS THAT SHADOW PLEASE

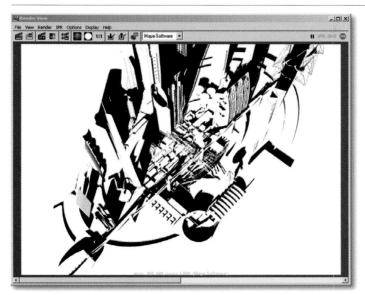

Even though the previous tip may be more trouble to set up than you might want to deal with, a separate shadow pass is frequently useful for standard rendering, as the capability to blur them or composite them separately over live action backgrounds is always useful. Various methods can be employed to achieve this, but here are a few: First, the Render Passes control mentioned previously works well, but it creates the shadow in the alpha channel. Next, clever use of a shader's Matte Opacity can give matting results that can leave shadows on white surfaces. Lastly, the Use Background shader is very useful for shadow passes when the background is set to white and the shader is assigned to all surfaces. This same shader is useful for simple composites where the live action background plate is set up as an animated image plane and receives shadows from objects reconstructed from and matching the plate.

   STRIKING A CHORD LENGTH

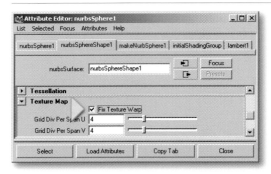

UV texturing is now replacing NURBS parameterized texturing because polygons are once again in vogue. One benefit of UV texturing is the texture can be totally unrelated to surface idiosyncrasies (although at a high labor cost in manually setting it all up). If you choose to take the easier road, texturing with NURBS, you may find stretching of the texture from the varying parameterization of the modeling. An easy fix for this is to select the object, and then in the Attribute Editor under Texture Map, choose Fix Texture Warp. This will spread the map evenly according to chord length, resulting in a consistent mapping.

   GLOW FLICKERING NO MORE

Nothing is more annoying than investing hours of rendering and having your shader glow flicker like there is an ensuing California power brownout in your scene. There are a few fixes for this, however. First, render a still frame with satisfactory glow settings in the Render View, and then in the Attribute Editor of the Multilister shaderGlow, disable Auto Exposure. Now look at your separate Maya Output window and put the Glow and Halo Intensity Normalization Factors values into the Glow and Halo Intensity fields. If any flickering continues on very small objects, select the geometry and, in the Attribute Editor, increase the Shading Samples under Render Stats. If only California had it this easy.

DETERMINING TEXTURE RESOLUTION

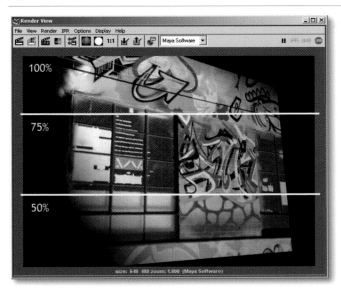

A dilemma has existed through the ages about which texture resolution is proper for a project. Answers have been invoked from Ouiji boards and Magic 8 balls, but the solution is really quite simple. 3D rendering is effectively all matrix calculation, where the color of a pixel is determined from the relation of various spaces, such as object or screen space. A texture map should ideally match the screen space of what it occupies in the render, but animation and perspective alter that simplicity. A good rule of thumb is to find the nearest proximity of the texture in relation to screen resolution and then scale down the resolution 75 percent. Texture aliasing should be avoided like mad cows, so shooting a bit smaller than screen resolution will ensure some stability in the texture, which will get visually crisper in animation anyway. Also, smaller textures equals less RAM and shorter render times, which equals happier producers and clients—who knew texture resolution could ultimately lead to world peace?

SAMPLER INFO FACING RATIO MANIA

This rather clunky sounding term can bring your shaders up more than a few notches. Facing Ratio is a method of deriving values on a surface as the normal faces or swings away from camera. This value can be used for example for increasing reflection as a window rotates away from camera (known as the fresnel effect). Creating rim lighting, transparent ghost-like edges, or x-ray glow effects are other common uses depending on what channel Facing Ratio is applied to. To use it, create a Utility Node called Sampler Info in the Work Area in the Hypershade panel. Next, create a Ramp Texture and delete the place2dTexture icon. Now MMB drag the Sampler Info over the Ramp and choose Other to bring up the Connection Editor. Pick Facing Ratio in the left column and connect to Uv Coord, V Coord in the right column. Now MMB drag the Ramp Texture onto the attribute of choice in your shader. Change the Ramp Texture to grayscale and IPR render in the Render View. Next, alter the Ramp Texture distribution to good effect. Now use the Creative Ingenuity button and apply throughout your project.

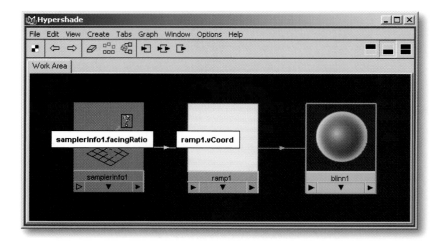

RENDER SCRIPTS RULE!

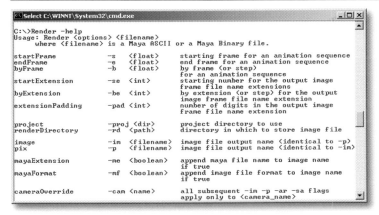

Most Maya users are taught to use the Render View for still render evaluation and Batch Rendering for animations. A much better way to render strings of frames is from the command line render. Open a DOS shell by going to Windows Start, Run and typing `cmd`. Look at your command line options and flags by typing `Render -h`. This will return back a flood of usage descriptions. Next, open Notepad and type a string following `Render <options> <your_scenefile.mb>`. Commonly used flags are `-s start_frame`, `-e end_frame`, `-b by_frame`, `-p output_file_prefix`, `-cam camera_name`, `-x X_resolution`, `-y Y_resolution`, `-of output_format`, `-pad padding_digits`, and `-n number_of_processors`. Note that there are also commands not found in the Render Global GUI such as `xLeft`, `xRight`, `yLeft`, and `yRight` for rendering sub-regions. An example might be as follows: `Render -s 1 -e 10 -b 1 -p Foo -cam persp -pad 4 -n 2 -x 720 -y 486 -of tif my_scenefile.mb`. This would render Foo.0001-10.tif. The advantage here is that you can shut down the Maya session to take full advantage of RAM and CPU cycles. If you want a record of the session to check RAM load, render times, and so on, you can pipe the output verbiage into a file by appending `> outfile.txt` after the render command in the text file. Lastly, suffix your text file with `.bat` to create an executable file and double-click when you're ready to rumble.

LAYERED SHADERS TO GO

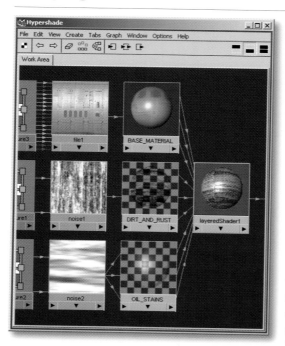

Perhaps the biggest workhorse of all shader models is the Layered shader. It is in fact not a shading model at all but is a very handy method of ascribing multiple shading models to a single surface. More than just a way to lay dirt or decals over a base surface, it can be used to create very complex shaders by mixing various shading models, such as Anisotropic, Lambert, and a Ramp shader all on one surface together. It is conceptually an "onion skin" of shaders piled on top of each other, with respective Transparency attributes revealing each in succession. To create a Layered shader, first create the shaders you want to layer. Next create a Layered shader and MMB drag each of your component shaders alongside the default green base. After you have brought them all in, you can delete the default layer and rearrange the layers as you like by MMB dragging them into a new order. The uppermost of the stacked onion skin will be at the far left. It is helpful to name each shader with a descriptive name to avoid confusion. Now render in IPR and modify each layer's transparencies with holdout maps to create a work of art (hopefully). Standard uses for Layered shaders are for rust or barnacle buildup, oil stains, billboards on a wall, and so on, but the sky is truly the limit as always in 3D. One drawback to Layered shaders, however, is that it will only use one displacement map if each shader has one assigned.

TO PREMULT OR NOT TO PREMULT

Premultiplication of alpha is one of those topics that cause endless confusion for many
Maya artists. Premult essentially deals with how Maya decides to anti-alias edges against a
background without knowing what the background really is. Maya premultiplies the RGB
images against a black background according to the alpha that is generated by the object.
This means that there is a slight black fringe of anti-aliased pixels surrounding every object
because it can only average the edge against a black background. If Maya knew what the
background plate was at the time of rendering, it could accurately create the anti-aliasing of
the alpha, but without it, all it can do is anti-alias against black. This does not pose a problem if your compositing package expects a premultiplied image, but some do not, and thus
a black halo appears around the objects. Shake and After Effects give you the option to un-
premult the image during import, which can also alleviate the problem. Maya by default has
Premultiplication turned on, but it is accessible in Render Globals, Maya Software, Render
Options, Color/Compositing, Premultiply. If turned off, Premultiply Threshold allows a variable amount primarily for gaming work. In general, you should leave it on, but check with
your friendly neighborhood compositor before committing an overnight render.

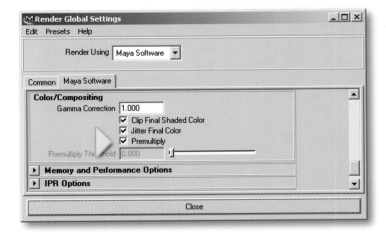

GETTING WET

Water tends to be one of the harder elements to faithfully re-create in CG. Behavior-wise, Maya Fluids begins to offer a solution for this slippery problem (sorry). But if you simply need to show a surface that appears wet or a good car paint appearance, there is an easy setup using Blinn shader attributes. In this shader, there is Specular Rolloff, which most tend to think only affects specular highlights. In fact, this attribute also affects reflection maps and raytraced reflection, the essential components of wet appearances. Specular Rolloff pushes the specular and reflection out to the edges away from camera normal, giving the appearance of wet edges. Raise the value from default .2 to around 3 or 4 and lower the Eccentricity down to .2 or so. You may need to raise the Specular Color to a value higher than 1 as well, perhaps 3 or 4. Lastly, remember that reflectivity should generally be no more than 1/Specular Color, so with a value of 4, the reflectivity should be set at .25.

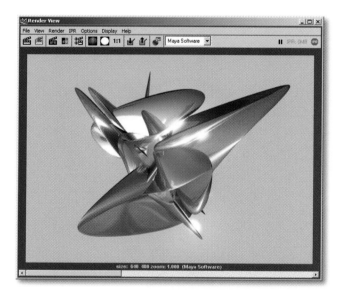

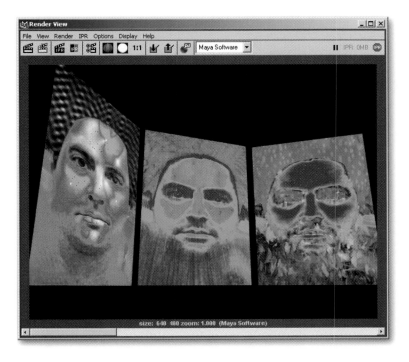

COLOR REMAPPING

Color Remapping is a great command that many pass up on their road to rendering. Color Remap is primarily used for replacing a texture's tonal range with one from another file's for surreal or abstract effects. For example, green alien skin can be made by remapping a facial skin tone map with lizard skin. The hue and value of the original file are remapped to a color ramp with hue assigned to U and value to V. The original color hue is lost as it connects to a V ramp, but new color values or textures can be substituted. Start with an image assigned to a File Texture, and then in its Attribute Editor, choose Effects, Insert Color Remap. A Ramp Texture is then displayed, altering the color of the original texture. Reduce the ramp to a black to white grayscale and observe that the tonal range is alterable similar to the curves function in Photoshop. Now add multiple sliders with various hues or textures mapped to them, and the fun begins. This is a great way to age, alter, or discolor existing maps or create a little psychedelia along the way.

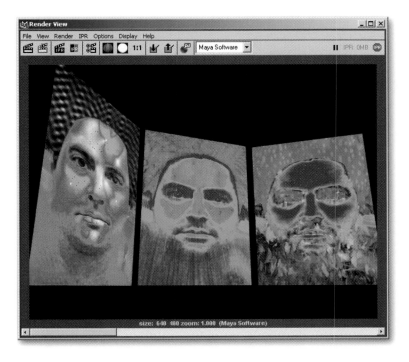

From Home Movies to Hollywood

*Lights, action, and CG camera!
Camerawork is another one of those
areas in which, without a little care
and affection, your work will unfortunately*

From Home Movies
to Hollywood

camerawork basics

*fall quite flat. Good camerawork, like charac-
ter animation, is a lifelong study, offering
much depth and range for what can be
learned and accomplished. In Hollywood, the
masters of camerawork are termed DPs, or
Directors of Photography. The art of cinema
that they have perfected is clearly the place to
begin to glean inspiration and technique. CG
camerawork, however, is odd in that it is not
bound to the physical world, and as such, it
has few of the imperfections and anomalies
that gravity and mechanics tend to leave as
signatures on Hollywood films. Much like
adding synthetic film grain and lens flares on
otherwise pristine CG imagery, we need that
imperfection to really have our brain feel that
the work is real and valid. As we accustom
ourselves to the precision of the digital aes-
thetic, perhaps this will fade, but for now
great attention should be paid to what the
legendary DPs have skillfully forged prior
to CG.*

RULE OF THIRDS

The first step in good camerawork is creating the composition of the image. You may be starting from storyboards where the basic layout is worked out already, or you may be creating and visualizing each shot directly in 3D. Whatever the case, the eye of the camera needs to be carefully considered by trying to establish a psychologically motivated point of view and dynamic tension of elements. Possibly the worst strategy is to dead center your subject, but there are DPs who can make even that succeed. It's better to reinforce a sense of depth of the 2D image by dividing up the screen into vertical thirds and placing a near ground object centered on one dividing line and a distant object on the other. This will establish field of view and dynamic tension with little effort. Of course good composition consists of much more than that and should weigh in factors such as emotion, color relationships, negative and positive space, tone, key, and narrative. Overall, good composition is pleasing, stimulating, or confounding and always leads the eye directly and gracefully to where the director intends.

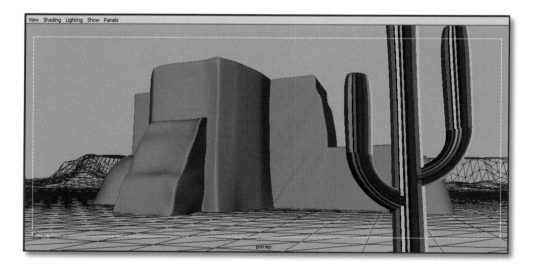

PERSPECTIVE BASICS

One of the ironies of computer graphics is that without prior training in the arts or design, many CG artists are never exposed to the principles of perspective because our software effortlessly calculates it in real time. Perspective is always considered the starting point for all artwork except in CG. Granted, many 3D artists acquire an innate feel for space and composition, but evidence of a lack of sensitivity to perspective abounds in the field. Developing a simple sensitivity to perspective is useful in arriving at a good composition, and it also shows a refined eye. The study of perspective is the analysis of vanishing points and how they fall within a frame. One-point perspective is simply a level camera with a single vanishing point at the center, usually in frame. Symmetrical and rigid in nature, it is usually best to avoid it. Two-point perspective is the most widely used by architectural delineators and photographers, as it introduces two vanishing points off either side of the image and maintains straight vertical lines. Three-point perspective allows full freedom of vanishing points, with two off either side and a third running up or down from the image. 3D packages operate in this mode naturally, but two point and single point can be achieved with proper camera orientation. A basic assumption is that if people's heads are aligned with the horizon line, it infers that the camera is at eye height above the ground. The next tip shows how Maya can be tricked into skewing the principles of perspective.

PERCEPTUAL PERSPECTIVE CORRECTION

A long-standing technique preferred by architectural illustrators and large-format photographers is to eliminate the third vanishing point while maintaining the position of the horizon line and key features. This amounts to effectively straightening out the converging vertical lines a camera would see as it tilts skyward. While looking upwards at a very tall structure such as a skyscraper, this phenomenon is unavoidable, but with lower structures, or even in a room, your brain compensates for the optical taper, keeping verticals parallel and delivering a perceptually correct view. You can test this out simply by tilting your head up toward the ceiling as you watch a corner of a room. Now do the same thing with a camera and observe the effect. Although the tapering is optically correct, being able to eliminate it in a 2D image such as a photograph or CG render creates a much more pleasing and refined look. Maya luckily has included the virtual analog of a perspective shift lens in a commonly overlooked attribute in the Camera Attribute Editor called Film Offset. Of little use in animated cameras (except for excellent abstraction potential), it shifts the virtual film plane in screen space x or y a given amount. To start, position a camera near the bottom of a tall building-shaped cube. Use the local camera command Panel View, Camera Tools, Yaw-Pitch Tool to then tilt upward, setting the horizon line at a given position. Next, under the Camera Attribute Editor, Film Back, Film Offset, type an arbitrary number such as .3 in the second field (y). The horizon will shift down below frame, but raise it back up to the same level with the Yaw-Pitch Tool. Now you will have the same view but with parallel vertical edges. If it is not yet parallel, try increasing or decreasing the Film Offset value and Yaw-Pitch accordingly. Your still renders can now look much more refined with this great technique. For something really wild, increase your field of view to a very large value and add Film Offset to both x and y. Now tumble the camera through your own version of Hitchcock's *Vertigo*!

PANEL VIEW VERSUS FILM BACK VERSUS RESOLUTION

Alias PowerAnimator, the original source for much of what is good in Maya, was one of the first packages to relate real-world optics and film properties to the virtual world of 3D cameras. Dubbed the Optical Toolkit back then, those functions now reside in Maya's Camera Attribute Editor. It basically consists of letting the user define a known film format around which to structure the 3D rendering, in effect placing film into the package. This makes integration with film or video immensely easier during compositing, but it does cause some confusion when relating the multiple viewing frames that a render can be interpreted through in Maya. First, go to Camera Attribute Editor, Film Back, Film Gate, and decide on an aspect ratio and format to work with, say 35mm 1.85 Projection. This will change your focal length (field of view), so enter, say, 63 in Camera Attributes, Angle of View. You still will not see the 1.85 letterbox aspect ratio in the viewing panel, so next you must apply a viewing gate there with Panel View, Camera Settings, Film Gate. Now a proper gate is visible, illustrating that the panel view is quite arbitrary but can hold a proper gating. If you want to enlarge the image and reduce the space around it, type 1.05 in Camera Attribute Editor, Film Back, Overscan. This function enables viewing of animation in and out of frame. Next, type the same aspect ratio resolution in Render Globals and now try Panel View, Camera Settings, Resolution Gate. It should show the same gating, indicating that you are all on the same page, from viewing panel to film back to output resolution.

   CREATING NATURAL CAMERA MOTION

Real-world camerawork has progressed from very static and slow movement to rapid cut, freeform handheld Steadicam-type movements. They both are shot from the aid of a human hand, and thus they have a distinctive, somewhat erratic signature. Perfectly-interpolated CG camera moves will always look artificial because we are accustomed to the imperfections of real cameras. A good way to create these inconsistencies and aberrations is to use a randomizer MEL script (randKey.mel is a favorite found on Highend3d.com) or manually set random imperfections to create small jitters and shakes in the camera action. Simply insert a selection of random keyframes on an already-established camera curve and then slightly randomize them to alter its perfection. If done subtly, a much more natural motion can be achieved, and the difference will be amazing—one camera movement feels human and one mechanical.

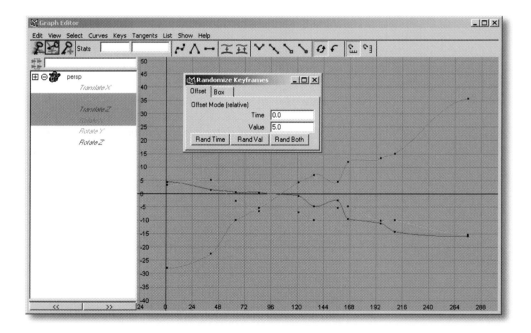

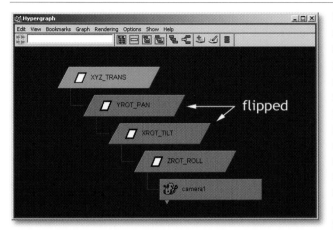

PROFESSIONAL CAMERA ANIMATION SETUP

Most casual Maya users animate the lower nodes of the camera grouping. This is the most expedient way to animate a camera, but a more robust and professional method is to use multiple nodes to hold animation channels. Start by creating a three-node camera with Create, Cameras, Camera, Aim, and Up. Open the Outliner window and group the upper node three times, then rename each node, starting with the upper, as XYZ_Translate, then the next one down as Pan or Yrot (if Y up is used), next down as Tilt or Xrot, and next down as Roll or Zrot. Note the sequence of rotation is YXZ, not XYZ, preventing gimbal lock. Next, select the camera with Panel View, Select Camera and lock all the channels in the Channel Box. This will prevent any camera tumbling or movement that could ruin the setup because the lower node must stay untransformed. Then begin the process of keyframing the camera's motions by translating or rotating the appropriate node in the chain. Remember to only set a key for the respective channel in each node, so you may elect to lock out all channels but the one to be keyed. This lengthy setup achieves an easily editable, channel-independent mode of camera control. If a slight increase in roll is desired, it is easily set and doesn't affect any other channels as a single node camera animation would, which is a great advantage in tweaking a move. Lastly, channels are well-organized in this fashion for easy import and export of curve data to other packages, motion control rigs, and so on. After learning this method, few people rarely go back!

CAMERA PROJECTION MAGIC

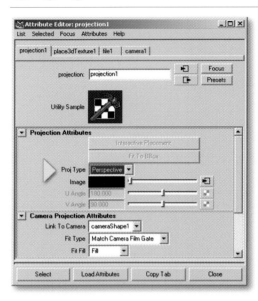

A major shift has occurred in the landscape (pardon the pun) of matte painting with the advent of 3D. Historically, complex background scenes that were prohibitively difficult to build used to be painted on glass, or more recently created in Photoshop, but are now projected into simple 3D layouts, enabling dimensional camera moves within the static painting. The technique used is that of camera projection, or using a perspective camera to project texturing information. Maya offers it as Perspective Projection, a projection type alongside the other standard types in the projection node, but it does requires a bit of careful setup to succeed. Camera projection is useful to more than matte painters because it is an excellent way to reduce the weight of a heavily-detailed model down to something that can be more easily painted. Tasks requiring the texturing of a huge number of parts can also be well-suited to this technique. Start with a collection of primitives and animate a camera pushing in, naming the camera Anim_Cam. Now study the parallax of the move and locate a point that maximizes the coverage of visible texture area. Copy the camera at that frame, strip out the animation, and name that camera Proj_Cam. Render a high-resolution 2k or 4k frame from Proj_Cam as a base for painting and then paint a color key over the various objects, assigning this file as a Perspective Projection map in a new shader's Incandescence channel. Assign all geometry to the shader and Choose Proj_Cam as the projecting camera under Camera Projection Attributes, Link To Camera. Now render a frame and check that the painting matches tightly to the geometry. If not, verify that the film back dimensions match the aspect ratio of the painting file. As the camera is now rendered throughout the sequence, you might find that this single projection may not be enough to properly texture all the surfaces that are revealed during the camera move. Surfaces that were partially behind other objects may display portions of the texture from the object in front. If this is the case, a second camera projection map for the occluded surfaces will be necessary, using alpha stenciling to paint in only what is necessary. This method is also excellent for dimensionalizing photography or 2D artwork. With a bit of practice, this is one of the great Killer Tips for Maya, so camera project on!

NO AUTO ANYTHING (ESPECIALLY CAMERA CLIPPING)

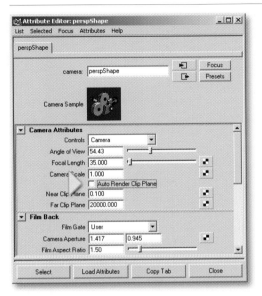

Automation is wonderful for such things as ATMs or the manufacturing of Twinkies. It is not so great when the success of your render depends on it. Maya includes an option called Auto Render Clip Plane in the Camera Attribute Editor that sounds like a good idea, but it can lead to indigestion and heartburn. It attempts to bind the clipping of the camera to the largest extent of the modeling, but because extreme clipping ranges are the number one source of render problems, it is wise to uncheck it and set clipping manually. It only takes a minute, and your happiness following a night's render may depend on it. For that matter, Auto-anything in Maya can lead to problems and is best avoided. Remember not to exceed the ratio of near clip at 0.1

and far clip at 20,000 because the math gets fuzzy, and your render is susceptible to artifacts. Pushing up the ratio a decimal place to 1 and 200,000 can be a fine strategy if a higher far clip is needed, or worst case, the scene can be scaled down.

SIMPLIFY, SIMPLIFY FOR ANIMATION

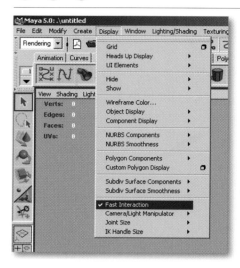

Thoreau must have foreseen computer graphics back in his day, because if there is anything that is NOT simple, it is CG. Fighting back complexity is the name of the game in 3D, and one of the areas that suffers from too much of it is camera animation. If there is too much density, resolution, or geometry in your scene, animating a camera can be unresponsive and difficult. Try these handy tips to fight the madness and get control of your camera. Start with the Panel, Show pull-down, and turn off unnecessary elements in the scenes such as deformers or CVs. In the same menu is Isolate Select, which enables temporary hiding of unselected objects, along with bookmarks. Next, turn on Display, Fast Interaction. This command draws objects in lesser resolution as they fall away from camera, speeding up responsiveness. Next, try wireframe versus shaded display mode, using the "1" display option for NURBS. Also try Window, Settings/Preferences, Performance Settings to disable any expensive deformation calculations during playback. Lastly, there is the old standby of turning objects to bounding boxes via Display, Object Display, Bounding Box. What worked in the eighties still works today!

UNDOS THE VIEWS

Often when doing camera animation, you create a view and later want to return to it. Rather than try to relocate the camera, there are handy keyboard hotkeys just for this—the bracket keys, [and]. One undos and the other redos the preceding views (just like a Seussian tongue twister). That is how we do our undos and redos of our views, sir.

FILM FORMATS FOR NEWBIES

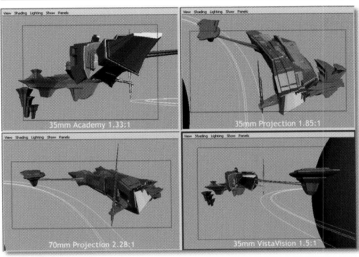

Film formats are a bit of a misnomer in CG because we don't really use film, but if you plan on doing feature film CG work, they are an inescapable fact of life. We adapt to the film world and not vice-versa, so Maya has a very convenient way to emulate film in the Film Gate settings in the Camera Attribute Editor.

The earlier tip, "Panel View Versus Film Back Versus Resolution," discusses how to set up the types listed, but these may be green to some who are new to the film world. Most theatrical releases are projected at a 1.85 to 1 aspect ratio, but that doesn't always mean it was shot that way. Also, a 2.28 to 1 aspect ratio is popular for epic widescreen features that might use a squeezing of the image as it is shot onto film that is unsqueezed at projection time, called an Anamorphic technique. Thus, Maya offers these various choices that a DP may make, which ripples down to the 3D visual effects artist. In the Film Gate options, 16mm choices are given but are rarely used. The common ones are the 35mm, especially 35mm Academy and 35mm 1.85 Projection. Academy is set at 1.33 to 1 and utilizes more of the celluloid area listed in the Camera Aperture fields in inches, but it is gated down in the theatre to a 1.85 crop. 35mm 1.85 Projection is useful when gating was used during shooting. The 35mm Anamorphic option is half of the 2.36 aspect ratio at 1.18 to 1, but it applies a Lens Squeeze ratio, resulting in thin vertical pixels. It is best avoided unless required for a show. 70mm Projection is commonly a 2.28 to 1 aspect ratio, and it creates a larger cinematic grandeur. VistaVision is next offered at a 1.5 to 1 aspect ratio with larger film back dimensions being 2 to 3 times the area of Academy. It is still commonly shot for visual effects plates. For the truly resolution-hungry, Maya includes Imax at a 1.34 aspect ratio and a whopping 2.7" × 2" area. Note the related resolutions for these sizes are set in Render Globals independently. Remember to set the proper lens Field of View as you change these because they alter the Focal Length.

   ANIMATED IMAGE PLANES GONE WILD

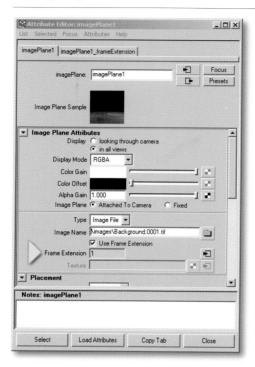

A handy use for image planes beyond that of a modeling tool is to use them as a rough compositor, adding the live-action background as a sequence to view your CG objects over or match elements to. The trick is to keyframe the extension of the file sequence and relate it to your timeline so that frames load in tandem with the CG animation. Begin by adding the first frame as an image plane and fit to your chosen film back or resolution settings. Now, under the Image Plane Attributes, check Use Frame Extension. You will note that moving the time slider makes no change, so we need to keyframe the extension into a curve. Set the slider to frame 1 and right mouse button on the Frame Extension field to Set Key. Now go to your end frame of the Image Plane sequence, enter that number in the Frame Extension field, and Set Key again. Now the time slider should update the background. Using the Select button at the bottom of the Attribute Editor will load this curve in the Graph Editor, where you can double the rate, cycle or oscillate the playback, and so on by manipulating the curve and resultant mapping of extension values to time.

WRESTING CONTROL OF FCHECK

Fcheck has had a GUI front-end for a while now, but to really wrest control of it, try running it from the command line. Open a DOS shell and type **fcheck -h**, then get ready for a lot of text return. You will find a veritable treasure trove of controls made available, mas-

sive amounts more than in the watered-down GUI. You might even locate the name of its creator at the end, Arnaud Hervas. The most commonly used flags are `-n start end by`, `-s scale factor`, `-m zoom factor`, and `-r frame rate`. With just those options alone, you can look at 2k images scaled down by 3 but zoomed back up twice playing on twos in order to fit into your available RAM. There are also controls to change gamma or color space and even write out a sequence in a new format. Hunt around the options and realize it is a terrific Swiss Army knife of RAM players.

IMAGE PLANE SPEEDUP

Maya can be run with garden-variety gaming graphics cards or expensive full-blown pixel-crunching work-

station cards. A lot of work can be done with the inexpensive gaming cards, but there are a few areas in which they come up short: performance of image planes and hardware plane functions such as Artisan and PaintFX. Hardware plane issues demand the better cards, but here is an easy fix for image plane slowdowns occurring from changes in Color Gain or Alpha settings of the image plane. You will need to add this line to your Maya.env file located in your Maya folder in the "Documents and Settings" folder on your drive: `setenv MAYA_SLOW_DRAWPIXELS 1`. This will dramatically speed up responsiveness on partial alpha background planes.

SNAPPING TO THE ELUSIVE CAMERA PIVOT

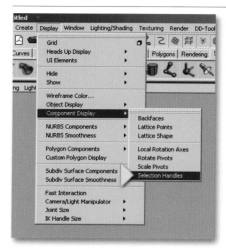

Often you may find yourself wanting to add something to an already animated camera, such as a flock of birds, a camera holdout matte, or a flying hot dog for a commercial. Grouping under a camera is easy, but often there are no points in which to snap to. To make the camera pivot visible and ready for snapping, start by selecting the camera and choose Display, Component Display, Selection Handles. Now a handle will appear that can be snapped to using the point snap mode.

STREAMLINING DEPTH OF FIELD

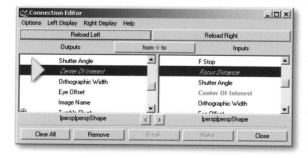

Camera depth of field is both a timeless emulation of optics as well as a trendy and transitory effect of the moment, similar to the lens flare boom years ago. There are many ways to achieve "DOF," some more accurate but expensive and some cheaper to render and less accurate. Maya integrates DOF in the Camera Attribute Editor under the Depth of Field menu. It is useful in that it provides a basic rendition of DOF for a bit of expense, but it is fairly tough to adjust the center of focus properly by guesswork. To make this step easier, we can use the Connection Editor to link two attributes in the camera. Start by MMB clicking on the camera icon in the Multilister or Hypershade. This calls up the Connection Editor, where we need to choose Center of Interest in the left column and Focus Distance in the right. Now if you select the camera and turn on the Manip Mode using the hotkey "t," you can adjust the Center of Interest manipulator to the area desired to be held in focus, and all is good in the world once again.

MOTION BLUR CHOICES

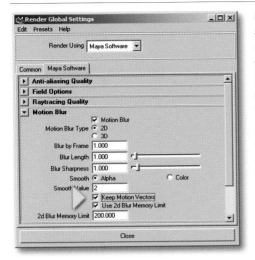

Motion blur is one of those seemingly minor aspects of rendering that is in fact one of the most important aspects of a renderer. In the film world, renderers live and die by motion blur performance and quality. In Maya, there are two choices—3D and 2D motion blur. 3D is much more expensive and artifact-prone render-wise but offers more realistic blur and control per object. 2D is a post-process that consumes significant RAM, but it is generally faster and preferable for most jobs. Another nice feature of 2D is the Keep Motion Vectors option in the Render Global Settings, Motion Blur menu. This enables a 2D post-process using the command line `blur2d` executable after rendering is complete in order to tweak the result. Type **blur2d -h** to see options in a DOS shell. Another nifty trick to use with standalone 2D motion blur is that you can use it to blur footage that was not rendered in Maya. Also, an invisible object in Maya still saves vectors, so if you have an image sequence mapped to the image plane, a totally transparent object with 2D motion blur can be used to smudge the image plane. You might also use this to smudge shadows that do not utilize motion blur or for some other kind of creative effect. The last option is to use a third-party motion blur application that inspects frames for 2D pixel travel and provides a reasonable alternative as well.

3D STEREOSCOPIC RENDERING

3D stereoscopic rendering seems to be the rage again for novel film experiences. Not since the fifties have we seen so many audiences wearing 3D glasses, except this time around they are wearing techy infrared full-color polarized glasses with surround sound on Imax screens. Who knew we'd have it so good. Of course, much of this revival is due to 3D rendering's ease of creating stereo imagery. Doing stereo animation properly requires a sophisticated camera setup in Maya and a decent method of playback and viewing, but here is an easy way to get your feet wet: First animate a camera over 8 frames with what would be a few inches to a few feet of spread from screen left to right. Render these 8 frames and use a handy Photoshop action called Anaglyph_Action.atn (found free online) to try frames 1 to 4 as left eye and 5 to 8 as the right eye to find the proper "interoccular distance" or eye spread. With that action, the red/blue compositing is done effortlessly and will deliver a beautiful result with red/blue glasses. For the next step, try a StereoJet polarized print for full-color rendition. Or go all the way and try a 3D remake of *House of Wax* on stereo Imax.

Building Character (Animation That Is)

ANIMATION

Character animation has led the charge in CGI evolution for several years now. It has driven ahead the explosive success of CGI in feature film effects, and the ambition to create persuasive and

Building Character (Animation That Is)

more than skin-deep

Contributions by Erick Miller

compelling human performance remains the Holy Grail that drives animators and directors forward. Conversely, the success of a 3D package in the market has largely hinged on how well it has supported this aim by providing tools of sufficient depth and flexibility for character work. Hands down, Maya overtook the industry so rapidly by providing a very flexible and rich toolset squarely aimed at the goal of supporting the complexities and vagaries of character animation. However, character animation is one of the more technical and involved subjects to learn in Maya, and therefore it does require a deep capacity to embrace technical issues and minutia. As an entrance test, you might ask yourself if 12:00 is flashing on your home VCR—if not, that is a good sign that you should venture forward. Doing character animation well is also a lifelong study because the technical issues are only the means to an end. The following tips should assist you in this journey into the deeper waters of Maya.

GETTING ORIENTED WITH YOUR JOINTS

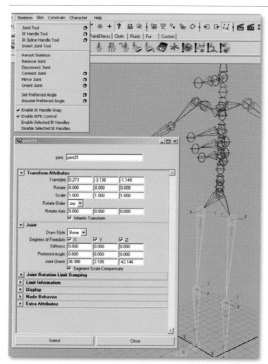

Creating joints is the way you build a skeleton for a character so that your character can transform from a rigid model into an animated character. To make joints, go to Skeleton, Joint Tool. You can start creating a portion of your character's skeleton by clicking in the view port with the Joint Tool and using the middle mouse button to lay the joints in the exact spot you want them. You can then create new portions of the skeleton and parent them to the appropriate joint by selecting the child and then the parent and hitting the "p" key. After you have laid out your character's skeleton, it is vital that the orientation of each joint is appropriate for the type of joint that it may be on the character's body. For example, the hip joint, which rotates the entire leg upwards and around, should have its rotation axis oriented in such a way that one axis points forward in front of the character, and the other points to the side. You can edit the local rotation axis of the joint by selecting the joint, going into component mode (hit the F8 key), right-click selecting the pick mask that looks like a question mark, and choosing Local Rotation Axes. You can then edit these components by selecting and rotating them. After you have them oriented perfectly to your liking, be sure to select all your joints and execute the MEL command in the command line:

```
joint -e -zso -ch;
```

This will align all your scale orientations with your rotate orients, which is quite important if you ever want to scale your joints. Finally, you want to try to avoid gimbal lock as much as possible. Gimbal lock is the phenomenon common to Euler rotations, when two rotation axes get lined up perfectly with each other and cause you to lose an axis of rotation. A good start to fighting gimbal lock is to set your rotation to gimbal mode by double-clicking on the Rotate Tool from the Toolbox and choosing gimbal. Next, open up the Attribute Editor for each joint and experiment with different rotate orders by clicking under the Transform Attributes section of the joint and choosing different rotate orders from the drop-down selection menus. To get the best rotation order least likely to cause the character to get into gimbal lock, simply rotate the joint and see if a 90-degree rotation causes the other two axes to get lined up with each other. If it does, then try a new rotation order.

FK, IK, OK?

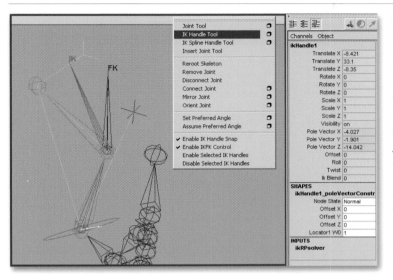

IK, otherwise known as Inverse Kinematics, is really not as complicated as it sounds. In fact, it doesn't really get any simpler! IK handles just enable you to attach a control to, say, an arm or a leg, which then creates a handle that you can grab and animate with. After you create an IK handle, you can translate the hand or foot around, and the angles of all the parent joints rotate into proper resulting positions—that's the mathematical calculation being performed by the IK solver. IK is great when you want to lock a hand or foot down onto a location and have the rest of the skeleton animate around it, like, for example, if a character was on the ground doing push-ups. The new IK handles in Maya 5 are quite versatile and interesting. To create an IK handle, go to the Skeleton menu and select IK Handle Tool. Next, simply select the parent joint (shoulder) and then the child joint (wrist) of your character, and an IK handle will be created automatically. The built-in capability to blend from IK to FK is a part of the new solver and is an addition that seems quite promising. To blend from IK to FK, simply change the attribute "IkBlend" from zero to one. You can then animate in FK mode of the skeleton by simply selecting it and setting keys. One other thing that is really important when dealing with IK setups is stable control over the center joint (elbow). You can always animate the twist attribute on the IK handle, but often times it is better to have a control there that you can select and animate. You can create a control for the center joint by creating a locator and positioning it somewhere on the side that the center joint bends toward, and then selecting the locator first, then the IK handle, and choosing Constrain, Pole Vector.

SMOOTH SKINNING HOTKEYS FOR PAINTING WEIGHTS

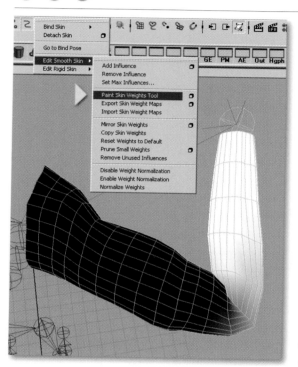

After you have set up and rigged your character, it is time to make it deform. Smooth skinning is the better, more sophisticated binding tool of choice (Skin, Bind Skin, Smooth Bind), but painting the weights of your smooth bound character can be more like wading through an endless sea of joint names. But, it doesn't have to be that way! There are a few quick tips and Artisan hotkeys that will, without a doubt, speed up your weight painting efforts. First, always remember that you can paint or assign weights on a per-vertex level simply by selecting the vertices of the geometry and then entering the paint weights tool (Skin, Edit Smooth Skin, Paint Skin Weights Tool). When you're within the tool, you can use the Flood option to fill all the vertices you have selected with a single value. You can therefore weight single vertices this way, without the painful old-fashioned way of having to open up the Component Editor, sort through the long, ugly list of vertices, and then type numbers by hand. Second, there is a great set of already defined Artisan hotkeys for painting that saves huge amounts of time, stream-lining the weight painting process. Here are some really helpful ones:

- Right-click over a joint and choose Paint Weights to paint weights for that joint. No more scrolling through an endless list of confusing joint names!
- Hold down the "u" key and left-click to choose your painting mode.
- Hold down the "n" key and left-click and drag to activate a virtual slider to change your painting value (between zero and one).
- Hold down the "b" key and left-click and drag to change the brush size.

After you get used to painting weights on a per-vertex level and using these little-known default Maya hotkeys, your ease and speed of painting weights should be quickly increased.

PLEASE CONSTRAIN YOURSELF

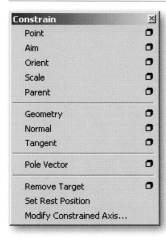

Constraints could easily be one of the most commonly used rigging tools, second only to Joints and IK. One of the slickest ways to control an object with constraints is to take advantage of the fact that constraints are weighted, meaning that each constraint of the same type (point, orient, and so on) on an object gets averaged with the other constraints of that type, based on each one of the constraint weights. If a constraint weight is zero, then that constraint has zero influence or control. If a constraint weight is one, then it gets equally averaged with all the other constraints. You can easily achieve a blending effect from one object to another by having two constraints and simply animating one of the weight attributes from one to zero and the other weight attribute from zero to one at the same time. There are many uses for such a technique, such as blending between multiple skeletal setups, like from an IK setup, into a special dynamics setup, and then perhaps into a motion capture setup. Another great use for blending constraint weights is to pick up objects and attach them to a character's hand or body. Constraints always operate as though they are in world space; that means that if you ever have a node that is being controlled by a parent transform, the constraint will take precedence over the parent. Point and orient constraints also have a relatively new attribute called Offset. By using the constraint's offset attribute, you can layer additional motion on top of the constraint in an additive manner, which lets you offset the constraint to any position you need. So, multiple constraint weights are the way to go. Whenever you need to blend from one transform space to another, don't dismay, constrain!

   NOT YOUR GRANDFATHER'S UTILITY NODES

While setting up a character, chances are that at some point you will find yourself needing or wanting to add some simple math into your character rig. Your first instinct may be to open up the Expression Editor and pound out a quick little expression that perhaps multiplies or adds two values and then maybe divides them by another. Traditionally, using expressions would be the way to go, but there are a few disadvantages with expressions that can become obvious over time. For one, the hard-coded node names that get embedded inside of expressions can potentially cause them to break when the nodes get renamed. Second, they can be a bit slow, depending on what they are calculating, because they need to be evaluated on the fly. So, what is a good solution? Use utility nodes! Those very same nodes that for some odd reason are labeled only for rendering can prove to be a character setup artist's best friend. Go to Window, Rendering Editors, Multilister. When the Multilister is open, go to Edit, Create. When the Create Render Node window is open, click on the tab furthest to the right, titled Utilities. Beneath this tab is a plethora of hidden treasures for character setup. Just to get started, there's the plusMinusAverage node, the multiplyDivide node, and the vectorProduct node, all of which immediately give you the capability to calculate all sorts of vector math, such as dot products and cross products. The condition node, the reverse node, and the clamp node can also prove quite handy in times when one would otherwise resort to bulky expressions. The time has now come for the world to recognize the immense power of utility nodes as character setup tools!

SQUASH AND STRETCH EXPRESSIONS

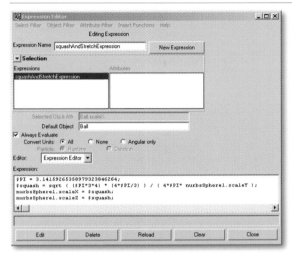

In this example, we will create a simple expression that uses a function for maintaining elliptical volume. One of the first rules for writing fast and efficient mathematical expressions for character setup is that you never want to directly evaluate MEL procedures that will hook data into your rig through an expression. You *can* do this, but it is much better to do straight variable assignment to attribute values. Doing this causes the expression node to actually create incoming attribute connections to the nodes that you are using to retrieve values in the expression. For example, doing something like this in an expression:

```
$value = nurbsSphere1.scaleX;
```

causes the expression node itself to connect the `scaleX` attribute of the sphere directly to one of its internal input attributes (`.input[ 0]` in this case). This is desired behavior because the expression node itself can keep track of the data as direct attribute connections between dependency data and doesn't need to perform as much evaluation in order to output the math within the expression. Try not to call a `getAttr` from within an expression (unless you are prepared for some potential problems, such as name changes that break the expression and create sluggishness). Of course there are some perfectly valid times to use heavy MEL within an expression, but for attribute assignment to variables, never use `getAttr` if you don't need to. Here is a simple example of integrating a simple formula into a mathematical expression. Notice the differences between expressions and MEL, such as variable type definition and direct attribute assignment being tied to variable definitions. Also note the direct use of the variable name in the square root function; it is not necessary to call `getAttr` because the expression will automatically calculate the attribute value internally much faster by using the attribute name directly. So, try this out:

```
sphere;
$PI = 3.14159265358979323846264;
$squash = sqrt ( ($PI*3*4) * (4*$PI/3) ) / ( 4*$PI* nurbsSphere1.scaleY );
nurbsSphere1.scaleX = $squash;
nurbsSphere1.scaleZ = $squash;
```

Next, try to scale the sphere along the Y axis using the `.scaleY`, which is the attribute that drives the expression. Expressions can be extremely powerful for character rigging when used properly.

SCRIPTING YOUR SETUP

```
Script Editor                                              _ □ ×
File  Edit  Script  Help

select -r baseSpineJoint.rotatePivot endSpineJoint.rotatePivot ;
string $result[] = `ikHandle -sol ikSplineSolver`;
string $cvs[] = `ls -fl ($result[2]+".cv[*]")` ;
for($cv in $cvs)
{
        cluster $cv;
};
// Warning: Some items cannot be moved in the 3D view. //
select -cl  ;


select -r baseSpineJoint.rotatePivot endSpineJoint.rotatePivot ;
string $result[] = `ikHandle -sol ikSplineSolver`;
string $cvs[] = `ls -fl ($result[2]+".cv[*]")` ;
for($cv in $cvs)
{
        cluster $cv;
}
```

MEL Scripting is useful in so many ways. One of the really great ways to use MEL is to create MEL scripts that auto-mate the character setup process. What this means is to create macro style scripts that call built-in MEL functions as well as other MEL scripts that have been written with the sole purpose of performing the character setup process. The benefits of creating an automatically scripted setup are two-fold. First, the process of rigging can sometimes be complex and confusing and is often quite involved, but if you script the setup, you can always have that script available to go back to or to reuse in other cases. Second, scripting the character setup should be done in such a way that if the geometry or even the joints that are being set up change later, the automatic scripted setup will still work. This means that even if the character changed drastically after you set it up, the setup itself would not need to change. This is a huge time saver, especially if the character runs the risk of needing a redesign that would otherwise force a redesign of the rig as well.

A very simple example of creating a scripted setup would be taking a set of joints, adding a spine IK to them, and then creating a cluster for each CV on the spline IK curve:

```
select -r baseSpineJoint.rotatePivot endSpineJoint.rotatePivot ;
string $result[ ]  =  `ikHandle -sol ikSplineSolver`;
string $cvs[ ]  =  `ls -fl ($result[ 2]+".cv[ *]")` ;
for($cv in $cvs)
{
cluster $cv;
```

BULGING BICEPS WITH SCULPT DEFORMERS

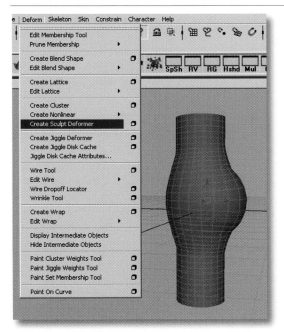

Sculpt deformers are one of the coolest non-linear deformers in Maya because of their stable, yet extremely fast and dynamic-looking layered deformation capabilities. Sculpt deformers are best to use on layered skinned characters or layered on top of geometry that is first deformed into place using some sort of linear deformer. The reason is that sculpt deformers can create interesting ellipsoidal bulging deformations across the surface geometry, but they will never give you the straightforward deformation that a joint bound to a skin cluster will when you are posing to a mesh. Instead, you can parent the sculpt deformer objects under the transforms of joints, scale the sculpt objects down to the proper size, and create all sorts of bulging effects using set driven keys or expressions that create the appearance of an object that is sliding beneath the geometry.

Create a polygon cylinder with enough resolution in the cylinder for it to deform nicely. Select the cylinder and then go to the Deform menu, Create Sculpt Deformer. Now, you should have a big bulge in your cylinder. Take a look in your 3D view and look at the nodes in the Hypergraph. You will see that there is a sphere-shaped sculpt object, and there is also a locator right at the center of the sphere. Select them both and scale them until there is a nice-looking bulge in your object. Now, play with some of the attributes in the Channel Box on the sculpt node. Maximum Displacement will cause a bulge that extends out more, and Dropoff Distance will cause a larger gradient between the origin of the sculpt object and its elliptically extended borders. The locator that is created is best kept as a child of the sculpt sphere, exactly at the center of the sculpt object, although slightly offsetting it can cause some nice angular sliding. Thus, this is just a general rule and is meant to be broken to create certain effects. Also note that NURBS geometry can be used as a sculpt deformer, which adds further possibilities.

     BLENDSHAPE FACIALS

Setting up blendshapes for facial animation is a process that can take thoughtful planning as far as what the shapes should be to get controllable facial targets. When setting out to model facial targets to create blend shapes, think about how the shapes will layer with each other. At the heart of a blendshape is a really simple, entirely linear and additive equation. It takes each vertex point position being blended in and first subtracts it from the original position to calculate an offset. Next, it just multiplies that offset by the weight value that is meant to be animated and then literally adds all the values together with all the other weighted offsets from the other shape models that are currently connected to the blendshape. Although this yields a straight line from vertex position to vertex position, it also yields an extremely predictable and appealing result. With this in mind, think about the shapes and how they layer together when setting out to model blendshapes. Here is a good list to start from when modeling face shapes. Each one of these models can and should most likely be split up into left, right, upper, and lower, depending on the shape itself and the portion of the face it affects:

- **Phonemes:** Aah, Eee/Iii, Ohh/Oow, Fff, Sss, Ddd, Gga, Cha/Shh

- **Emotions:** Happy/smile, sad/upset, angry, annoyed, disgusted, surprised, confused

- **Additive separate shapes:** Brow up/down/furrow, blink, eyes wide/squint, snarl, nose flare, cheek up/down/toward center/away from center, lip pucker/flattened/squashed together, each lip up/down/toward center/away from center, each lip curl in/out, each corner up/down/toward center/away from center, entire mouth slanted side to side

As you are modeling each shape, it is important to test how they work with each other, which is a vital part of modeling face shapes. Finally, remember that when you add blendshapes into a model that is already deforming (say with a jaw joint for example), be sure to use the Deformation Order option from the Blendshape Options window in the Advanced tab and set it to Front of Chain.

WRAP DEFORMERS

The purpose of a wrap deformer is to use a lower resolution mesh to drive the deformations of a higher-resolution mesh. This way, you can do many things much faster, such as skinning, weighting, and making updates to the final high-resolution geometry, all without affecting the actual weights that have been painted or the vertex ordering of the final deforming mesh. Wrap deformers' only drawback is that they can be somewhat slow to calculate, especially on the initial binding calculation for a high-res mesh. First, create a polygon cylinder, with settings of Subdivisions Axis at 20 and Subdivisions Height at 10. Next, create a lower resolution cylinder, this time setting the Subdivisions Axis to 8 and Subdivisions Height to 3. Now, delete history and freeze transformations on all. Next, use Skeleton, Joint Tool, and put the lower joint at the bottom of the cylinders, the center joint at the center of the cylinders, and the top joint at the top of the cylinders. Finally, bind the low-resolution cylinder to the joints using smooth skinning (Skin, Bind Skin, Smooth Bind), being extra careful not to select the higher-resolution mesh when you perform the bind. Select nothing, then select the high-resolution mesh first and the low-resolution mesh second, and then perform Deform, Create Wrap. You should now have a wrap deformer that you can play with that should deform the higher resolution mesh by rotating the joints on the lower resolution mesh. Finally, you can tweak some of the attributes to get a performance gain on the wrap deformer. For example, you can set the Weight Threshold attribute value all the way to one. This will sacrifice the nice, smoothed, rounded deformations on the high-resolution model, and in places low-resolution edges will bend, but it will increase performance of the wrap deformer itself by quite a bit. You also can tweak Max Distance, which is the maximum distance that the deformer should use to determine how far away the low-resolution object will ever be from the high-resolution object at the time the wrap deformer node is created. Tweaking this attribute to its bare minimum can also improve performance on the wrap deformer.

FLOWING DOWN THE PATH

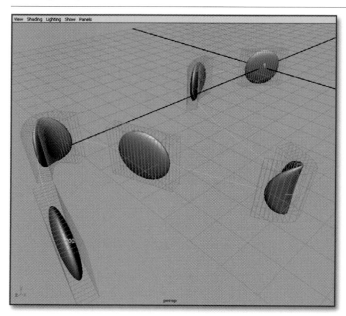

A common animation technique is to set an object to a motion path to choreograph its translation. A not-so-common variation of this technique is to use Flow Paths, a nifty trick where a lattice is translated along with the object, but whose local axes of each set of points follows the curve, thus deforming along the way and influencing the host object as well. This is clearly useful for fish swimming but can be applied to any squash animation technique. Start by creating a NURBS sphere and scaling z at .2. Draw a CV curve that contains some sharp corners originating at the sphere location. Rotate the sphere in y with the slender side aligned with the curve. Next, select the sphere and then Shift-click to select the curve. Choose Animate, Motion Paths, Attach to Motion Path options. Make sure Follow is checked, orient the Front Axis to x, and then choose Attach. Play it back to check proper path animation. Now select the sphere then curve again and choose Animate, Motion Paths, Flow Path Object options. Choose 10 Front Divisions and press Flow. Now the sphere will follow the contours of the curve. Note that the options enable the lattice to be attached to the object or the entire curve for very precise deformations.

CYCLE THOSE CURVES

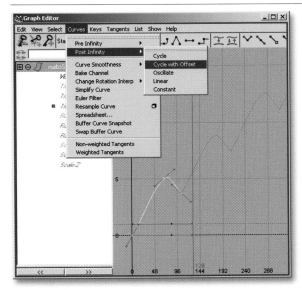

In the Graph Editor, curves are manipulated to establish the animation of an object. One way to reduce the setting of redundant keys involves using the cycle options in the Graph Editor. Create a few basic keys on a curve and then choose Graph Editor, Curves, Post Infinity, Cycle. The curve will repeat indefinitely, but to view it, choose Graph Editor, View, Infinity. Now try the other options such as Linear, where the final tangent is shot into infinity, enabling two keys anywhere in time to establish speed. The option of Cycle with Offset will cycle but stack the next on top of the last, creating an escalating effect.

   ## FREE THEN BREAK YOUR TANGENTS

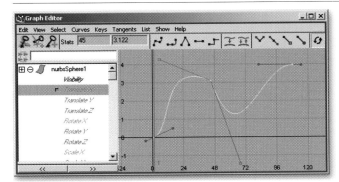

Getting good results by simply manipulating keys in the Graph Editor can often be good enough, but to really provide subtle control over your motion, use the full array of tangent tools available. Start by creating a few keys, then select the curve and choose Graph Editor, Curves, Weighted Tangents.

This will enable more precise control over what are normally simple tangent handles. Next, select a key and then select Keys, Free Tangent Weight as well as Keys, Break Tangents. Now each tangent handle is controlled much as a Bézier curve is in illustration packages. Not only is this method more intuitive, but it also can be used to create very subtle or dramatic curves that the default methods cannot.

FLAP YOUR WINGS WITH EXPRESSION

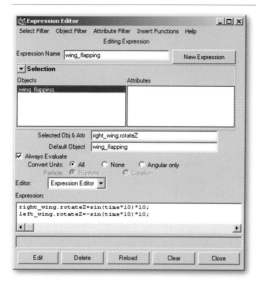

If you are new to expressions, here is a good introduction to them and a reason that you might use one—that of a bird flapping its wings. For our example, we will use simple spheres, but feel free to consult your local Audubon Society chapter for modeling help. Start by constructing three spheres, one rounded for the body and two flattened for wings. Locate the pivot points of the wings just inside the body. Name the wings right_wing and left_wing and parent under the body node named Boid. Now open the Expression Editor under Window, Animation Editors. Call the Expression Name wing_flapping and insert this in the main expression field:

```
right_wing.rotateZ=sin(time*10)*10;
left_wing.rotateZ=sin(time*10)*10;
```

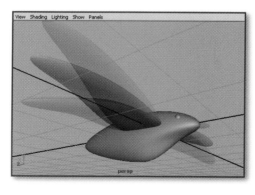

The first value of 10 is the rate of flapping (per second) and the other 10 is the amount of rotation in degrees. Change these to suit your preferences. To add an attribute that provides easier control and possible keyframing of this rate, pick the body node and under the Attribute Editor, choose Attributes, Add Attributes. Call the Attribute Name flap_speed and set Minimum to 0, Maximum to 40, and Default to 10. Now update the expression to this:

```
right_wing.rotateZ=sin(time*Boid.flap_speed)*10;
left_wing.rotateZ=sin(time*Boid.4flap_speed)*10;
```

Use the new slider in Boid's Attribute Editor, Extra Attributes to key or make other connections to other expressions.

GRAPH EDITOR EXPRESSIONS

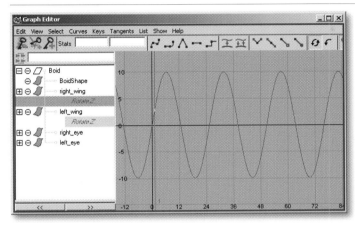

The Graph Editor offers access to keyframes primarily, but it does offer simple viewing of expressions, which can give useful information if needed. Select the Boid node created in the previous tip and open the Graph Editor. Choose View, Show Results. Open the hierarchy in the Graph Editor Outliner and select the RotateZ of either the left or right wing. A sine wave should appear, but note that it is not editable without using Curves, Bake Channel. Note also that some complex expressions may tax the Graph Editor, so the Show Results options offer different sampling rates for dealing with this issue.

FINDING THOSE RECLUSIVE LOCAL AXES

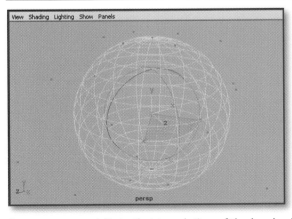

Here is a function that is hidden away in a nook that many may overlook. Frequently, a local axis may need to be oriented differently from default for animation purposes. There is no command for this, so here is how to do it: Select the object in question and then go to the Component mode selection menu. Right-click on the question mark to display the object's local axis. When selected, it is available for rotation through the standard Rotate command. Note that translation of the local axis is not available here because the local pivot would need to be altered (that is, the use of the Insert key) to allow for that.

   PROMPTING MULTIPLE KEYFRAMES

Here's a great little timesaver when you need to set many keys across a span of time. Go to Animate, Set Key Options and check Set Keys At Prompt. Press Set Key, and a small menu will appear that will enable you to input a range of individual frames to which you may set

keys. To determine to which attribute you are setting keys, use Set Keys on Current Manipulator Handle while the axis you are interested in is clicked on to be active.

   BREAKDOWN YOUR KEYS

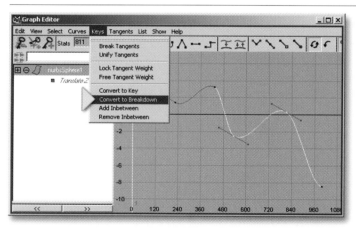

One handy feature in the Graph Editor you may have missed is the use of Breakdown keys. A variation of standard keys, Breakdown keys are keys put in a different state where they are influenced by the position and value of neighboring keys, making modification of sets of keys much easier. Begin with a curve containing multiple keys.

Select a few internal keys that have neighbors and then choose Keys, Convert to Breakdown or right-click over one to find the same command. Now select a neighboring key and move it in time and notice how the Breakdown keys respond by scaling appropriately. When done, convert back to standard keys with Keys, Convert to Keys.

DRIVING MISS DRIVEN KEY

Maya has a few tricks up its sleeve that other packages may not. One example of this is Set Driven Key, which essentially is expressions for lazy people. Not that that is a bad thing, of course. Set Driven Key simply connects one animated attribute to another so that one acts upon the other. It goes one step further in that it maps out that relationship to an editable curve so that the relationship between the two can be refined and optimized. Start by creating a sphere and a cube scaled into a long box. Raise the sphere above the cube and select the sphere. Choose Animate, Set Driven Key, Set options. While the sphere is selected, choose Load Driver, select the box, and select Load Driven. Highlight translateY of the sphere and rotateY of the box. Press Key, raise the sphere in Y, rotate the box a few revolutions in Y, and then press Key again. Now as you raise the sphere, it will spin the box rapidly. To edit the resultant curve, pick the box and open the Graph Editor. Now timings and eases can be set easily. Remember, the power in Set Driven Key is to link any number of attributes together in complex ways with relative ease.

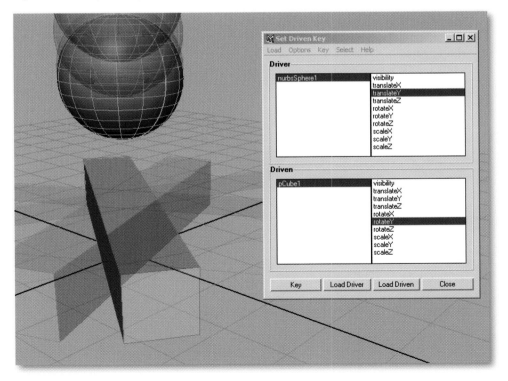

TEXTURE MAP YOUR ANIMATION

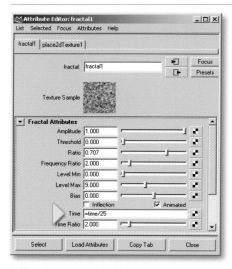

Here is a genuine Killer Tip for creating random functions from 2D textures for animation channels of objects. Start by creating a sphere and opening the Attribute Editor, as this hook will not be accessible through the Channel Box attribute fields. Right-click in the Translate Y channel field and choose Create New Texture. Pick a 2D Fractal Texture and turn on the Animated check box in Fractal Attributes. Playback of the timeline will not yet create motion, though, because we need to provide keyframing of the Time field or simply place a simple expression such as =time/25 directly into the field. After that is entered, play back for erratic motion. Now modulate fractal parameters such as Ratio for smoothness or Alpha Gain or Offset for intensity. Other options exist similarly with the 2D Noise Texture, which has interesting options such as Perlin, Billow, Wave, or the intriguingly named Space-Time.

TIME SLIDER TRICKS

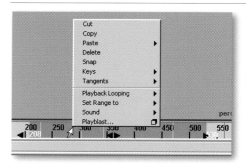

Setting keys in Maya is typically done by right-clicking to Set Key in an attribute field or perhaps by using the keyframe hotkeys such as "s" (key all keyable fields), Shift-W (key translations), Shift-E (key rotations), or Shift-R (key scaling). Many artists, however, fail to consider that the timeline itself offers various conveniences for keyframing. Start by Shift-clicking on a red key indicator in the timeline. Two arrows appear, enabling movement of the keys within the timeline and saving a trip to the Graph Editor. Now Shift-click on a collection of keys and note that new arrows are added in the outer edges to scale the collection in or out, while the inner arrows can translate all together. Lastly, move the slider to a red marker or keyframe that you want to delete and right-click to find a pop-up menu that has a variety of useful hidden functions, including delete. This will save gas and reduce time-consuming trips to your local Graph Editor.

RECORDING YOUR MOUSE

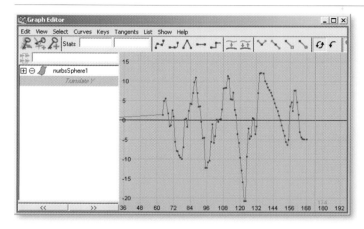

Here is a hidden gem tucked well away in Maya. Often it could be helpful to use mouse movement to create animation curves in order to provide a "hand-held" feel or establish erratic motion to objects or attributes. Deep inside MEL is a node called the Record Node that will facilitate such a trick. It is basically a node that will record mouse actions as keyframed curves and pipe those curves into an attribute of another node. After data is captured, the Record Node can be deleted. Start by entering this bit of MEL to set it up:

```
sphere;
createNode record;
connectAttr nurbsSphere1.ty record1.input;
```

Now set your playback speed in the Animation Preferences to 15 fps in order to avoid out-distancing the record process. Begin the capture with this command:

```
play -record;
```

Now move the mouse erratically in order to move the sphere in y translation. After a few seconds, use the Esc key to stop the recording and view the resultant curve in the Graph Editor. Other attributes can have concurrent connections as well to save cutting and pasting of curves. Bear in mind that the attributes chosen can be much broader than just translations.

Dangerous Effects Animation

Blasting
Zone
Ahead

Effects animation is the real underdog of visual effects work. When done skillfully, it is invisible to the viewer because the willing suspension of disbelief kicks in (hopefully), and the viewer believes he or she is simply viewing natural phenomena, as opposed to the reality of an agonizingly worked-out and tediously orchestrated CGI effect. Effects artists spend their lives working

Dangerous Effects
Animation
things you *can* do at home

Contributions by Eric Pender

hard at having complex events appear natural instead of man-made. It is diametrically opposed to character work, where the perform-ance is highly intentional and demands your attention. They do both seek to create com-pelling cinematic performances. Character animation strives for emotional response, whereas effects animation strives for a visceral response. The pod race explosions in Star Wars Episode 1 *or the dramatic plane crashes in* Pearl Harbor *remain as landmarks in arresting film experiences. Coincidentally, both of these were created primarily with the help of Maya dynamics. Known as a powerhouse for dynam-ics and particle work, Maya enables extremely robust re-creations of complex events. Similar to character animation, it remains as one of the deeper areas in the package to master, requiring patience and a cast-iron stomach for technical issues and minutia. These tips can be considered virtual antacids for the technical heartburn you may encounter along the way, and they also illustrate the depth and range of what is possible in Maya.*

DYNAMIC WINDOW LAYOUTS

Often you find yourself doing effects in between other tasks. It is often helpful to save a layout specifically for animating dynamically. Under Panels, Layout, select the Two Panes Side by Side layout. In the left pane, select Panels, Panel, Dynamic Relationships. This is like the Outliner window but enables you to connect and disconnect fields. To save the layout, select Panels, Saved Layouts, Edit Layouts, click the New Layout button, and finally change the name to something like Dynamics. Now, when you want to do some dynamic animation, select this layout to make the process easier.

USE PLAYBLASTING TO CHECK MOTION

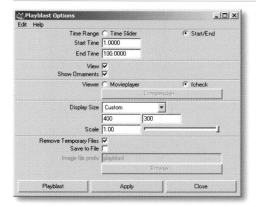

Many times with dynamic animation, it is easy to get fooled by the speed of the default timeline playback. It is simply not real time when you play the simulation according to the speed of the graphics card, even though card speeds today are formidable. As soon as you feel your animation is reasonable, it is best to check it with playblasting. In the main menu, choose Window, Playblast option box. Set your desired frame range, select Fcheck, make a guess at display size based on available RAM, and then press Playblast at the bottom. This will do a sequential hardware capture of the selected viewport and then play it back in Fcheck. In Fcheck, press "T" to play back in real time mode. Often your perception of your animation will be much different at the correct speed. Also remember to set Playback Every Frame in the Playback section of Animation Preferences to ensure proper simulation.

   ## A ONE-MINUTE OCEAN

You can now quickly create animated water. This used to be a very complicated task. Select the option box of Fluid Effects, Ocean, Create Ocean, choose Create Preview Plane, and complete with Create Ocean. Now add a Directional light pointing down. When you play the scene, the preview plane will move, and you can get a rough idea of the default motion. Change the values in the Ocean shader and render.

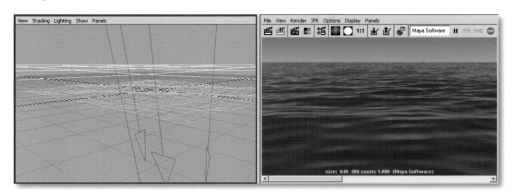

SOFT BODY ROPE TRICKS

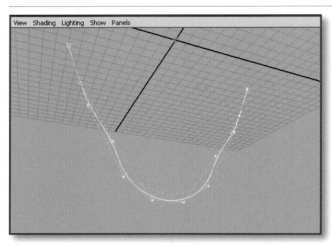

Rather than referring to the antics of an out-of-shape cowboy, this is actually a cool trick for animating a dynamic rope behavior. Make sure your grid is displayed and press the Snap to Grids option in the Status Line. Use the Create, EP Curve Tool to create a curve that is perfectly straight with each point on a neighboring point on the grid. Start on the left and click to the right one grid point over for an arbitrary ten units. Select the curve and from the menu choose the option box of Soft/Rigid Bodies, Create Soft Body. Under Creation Options, choose Duplicate, Make Original Soft. Click on Hide Non-Soft and Make Non-Soft a Goal. Set the weight to 1 and click Create. In the Status Line, press Select by Component Type and then select all the points in the curve except the two at either end. Press Ctrl-A to open the Attribute Editor and under the heading Per Particle Attributes, right-click in goalPP and select Component Editor. Select the Particles tab at the top, listing all selected points. Expand the window so that you see all the goalPP attributes. Click and drag from the top value to the bottom value of goalPP, press 0, and press Enter. All the selected points will now have a goalPP of 0, while the end points that we did not select will retain a value of 1. Close the window and then in the Status Line press the Select by Object Type button and select our original curve. In the menu, select Fields, Gravity. Reselect the curve and in the menu select the option box for Soft/Rigid Bodies, Create Springs. Change the Creation Method to Wireframe, the Wire Walk Length to 2, the stiffness to 10, and then press Create. Play the scene, and you can see how fun soft bodies can be. Experiment with spring stiffness and damping. Do a playblast to see it in real time.

ALL SOFT BODIES MUST REST

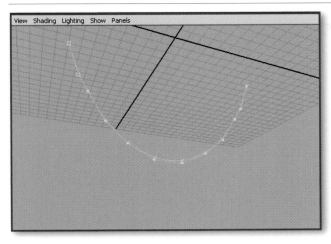

Let's now use the rope we made in the previous tip. Notice that it starts as a straight line and then falls and bounces around. As cool as that is, sometimes we want to do an animation that requires the soft body to start in a resting position. One way to get there is to set your frame range really high and play the scene until the object stops bouncing. Unfortunately, our particles have nothing to slow them down, so that can take a while, but there is a better way. Select the rope and then add Fields, Drag options. Set the Magnitude to 1 and the Attenuation to 0. By playing the scene, the rope will fall and then come to a rest rather quickly. Now, with the rope selected, choose Solvers, Initial State, Set for Selected. Rewind and then play the scene, and you will find that the rope is not moving, being in a nice resting state. Disconnect the Drag Field from the rope by selecting the curve in the Dynamics Relationship Editor and on the right side with the Fields button checked, turn off the dragField1 by clicking once on it. Now save the file under a different name and add Rest to the end of it, for example. This technique is useful for anything that hangs, such as curtains. Start your animation from the rest state and then add wind and turbulence to get it moving.

JUMP THAT ROPE

In the previous tip, the goal object we originally created is called "copyOfcurve1," to which the ends of the rope are attached. By containing the goalPP attribute of 1, it can still be really useful. So far we have simply used it to hold the rope still in space, but we may want the ends of the rope to move in space. Select the copyOfcurve1 and in the Channel Box, right-click in the Translation Z field and select Expressions. Enter this in the Expression field:

```
translateZ=8*sin(time*2);
translateY=8*sin(time*2);
```

Reconnect the drag field to our rope in the Dynamics Relationship Editor by selecting the original curve and then, on the right side, clicking on dragField1. Select dragField1, open its attributes, and change the Magnitude to .1. Make sure that your scene is set to play a lot of frames, perhaps up to 3000, and then hit play. The expression we put in the goal object will move the ends of the rope. Play the scene and let the motion develop. Now stop, rewind, and change the Stiffness setting of the springs to 20. Play the scene, and now the rope should work nicely after about 1000 frames. Notice how, when you change the stiffness of the springs, the reaction of the rope changes dramatically. Many times in dynamic anima-tion, you need to experiment with the many variables to find the sweet spot.

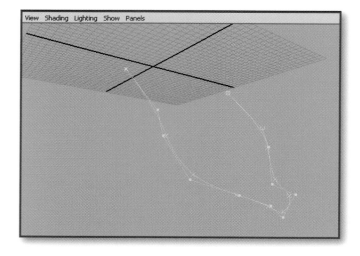

A SIMPLE RIGID BODY ANIMATION

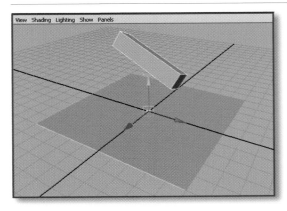

Often, learning a technique is a matter of experimenting with a very simple example and then applying what you have learned to larger examples down the road. Create a horizontal NURBS plane and scale it to 10 in all directions. Create a poly cube and raise it in Y 5 units. Select the NURBS plane and then select Soft/Rigid Bodies, Create Passive Rigid Body. Now select the cube and select Active Rigid Body. Next, with the cube still selected, choose Fields, Gravity. Play the scene, and you now have the most boring rigid animation possible. Rewind the scene, select the cube, and put a small amount of rotation on a few axes. Play the scene again and watch it get a lot more interesting. To adjust the way the floor or cube reacts, select the object, and then in the Channel Box you can change many variables such as Scale X to make a tube or Translate Y to add more height.

   ## A SIMPLE EXPRESSION TO MOVE A PASSIVE RIGID BODY

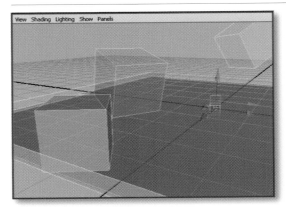

Using the same scene as the previous tip, let's modify it a bit with a powerful feature. In the Dynamics Relationship Editor, select the NURBS plane, right-click, and select Show Shapes. Click the cross next to the NURBS plane and then select rigidBody1. Press Delete, select the NURBS plane again, and then in the Channel Box, right-click in Translation Y and select Expressions. Enter this equation:

```
ty=.5*noise(time*3);
```

Press the Create button and then play the scene. The box will not hit the plane, but the plane will vibrate up and down. Now rewind, select the plane, and then make it a Passive Rigid Body again. Play the scene now, and you will see the box reacting to the movements of the plane.

   USING PARTICLES TO VISUALIZE NOISE VERSUS RANDOM

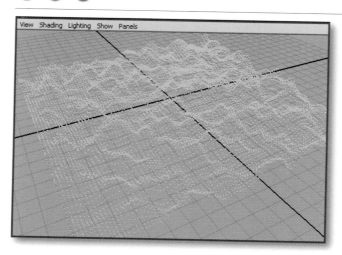

When you are new to effects, one important concept to grasp is the noise field. Some people describe it as random, but it is actually not quite random. It is more based on a predictable natural randomness, which can look like clouds or mountains depending on how you use it. Here is a simple way to visualize the difference. Make a grid of particles with the Particles, Particle Tool options. Turn on Placement, With Text Fields and then set the Minimum Corner to –10, 0, –10, the Maximum Corner to 10, 0, 10, and the Particle Spacing to .2. This will give you a plane of particles. Now select the Attribute Editor for the particles and under the Per Particle Attributes, right-click on Position and select Runtime Expression. Enter this:

```
position+=<<0,noise(position),0>>;
```

Play a single frame only by typing **2** in the current frame. Now you will see the particles raise or lower into a hilly pattern. Rewind the scene and replace the rule with:

```
position+=<<0,rand(1),0>>;
```

Now play one frame. Notice how the `rand` calculation is much more random while the noise is like periodic rolling hills.

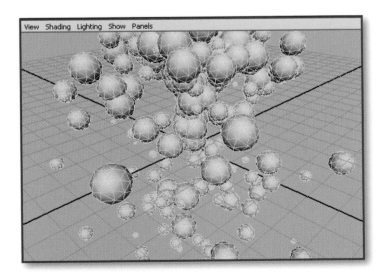

RANDOMLY SIZED PARTICLES

To create more variation of particle sizes, we will begin by making a simple fountain. Create an emitter in Particles, Emitter options and choose Directional in Emitter type. Set the direction to 0, 1, 0 in Distance/Direction Attributes, the spread to .2, and the speed to 10. Now select particle1 and choose Fields, Gravity. In the particle1 Attribute Editor, go to Render Attributes, Particle Render Type and select Spheres. Now choose General under Add Dynamic Attributes, bringing up a window with several tabs at the top. Select the Particle tab, locate radiusPP, select it, and press OK. Now right-click in the field next to Per Particle (Array) Attributes, radiusPP and select Creation Expression. In the Expression Editor, enter:

```
radiusPP=.1+.5*rand(1);
```

Now upon playing this you will have created particles that receive a different radius based upon the equation we entered in the Creation Expression field. The function `rand(1)` returns a random value between 0 and 1.

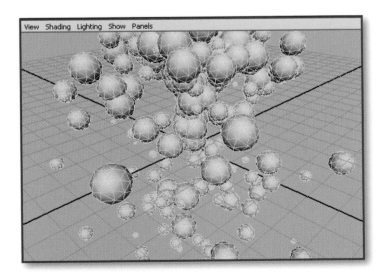

View   Shading   Lighting   Show   Panels

BIGGER PARTICLES FALL FASTER

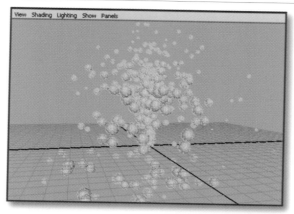

Now using what was created in the previous tip, let's make the larger particles fall faster than the small ones. In the particle1 Attribute Editor, right-click in the Per Particle (Array) Attributes acceleration field and select Runtime Expression. Enter this:

```
acceleration=10*<<0,-
particleShape1.radiusPP,0>>;
```

Before you play the scene, disconnect the gravity field from the particle in the Dynamic Relationships

Editor. Now the expression we entered in the Runtime rule controls how the particles fall. The smaller ones get very little gravity compared to the bigger ones. To enhance the scene further, adjust the equation to be:

```
acceleration=10*<<0,-particleShape1.radiusPP-.34,0>>;
```

PLAYBACK EVERY FRAME OR ELSE

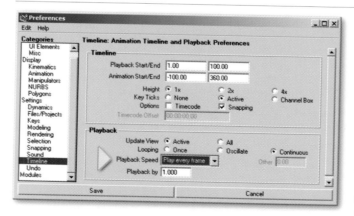

Particle simulation requires run-up, a cache of calculations that enables successive frames to properly compute. Normally this run-up is invisible to the user, but it does require that Play Every Frame is selected in Animation Preferences, Playback, Playback Speed. Odd behavior can be fixed by ensuring that this is set correctly; also remember to fully reset the playback to frame 0 before a new test.

MAKING PARTICLES COLLIDE WITH A FLOOR

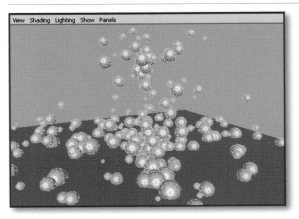

Let's use the same animation as in the previous tip but add a floor. Create a horizontal NURBS plane and scale it up to 30 units. Play a few frames so that you see the particles and the new NURBS plane in the viewport. Select them both at the same time. Now, in the menu, select Particles, Make Collide. To verify that it was done, go to the Dynamics Relationships Editor, select particle1, and then in the right column, click on SELECTION MODES, Collisions. You should see nurbsPlaneShape1 listed. It should also be highlighted, which tells you that the current particle will collide with this object. Now play the scene, but chances are, you have a problem. Your emitter, located at 0, 0, 0, is on the plane, so some particles get emitted up and others bounce down. A simple solution is to raise the emitter in Y until all the particles start above the plane. To change the behavior of the collision, select nurbsPlane1 and open the Attribute Editor. Select the tab called geoConnector1, ignore the Tesselation Factor, and adjust the Resilience that influences the bounce, as well as the friction that controls how slippery the plane is.

PARTICLE LOOPING

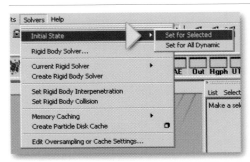

Often, particle effects can be useful to cycle repeatedly in order to create mapped 2D card replacements or rhythmic effects. In order to create a seam to provide temporal matching, select your particles on the last frame of the sequence and choose Solvers, Initial State, Set for Selected. Now the first and last frames will match, enabling seamless loops.

KILL PARTICLES WHEN THEY GO BELOW A CERTAIN HEIGHT

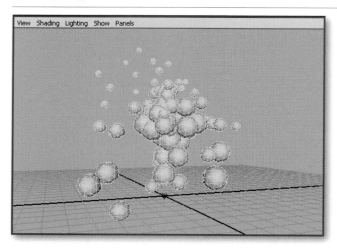

Continuing to build on the previous tip, let's kill the particles instead of colliding them. There can be many instances where you simply need to get rid of the particles instead of making them bounce. Fewer particles mean better performance, so getting rid of obscured particles will speed things up. Delete the plane that has the collision on it, open the Attribute Editor for particle1, and go to the Lifespan Attributes, selecting lifespanPP only in Lifespan Mode. Now in the Per Particle Array Attributes, right-click in the lifespanPP and select Runtime Expression. Add the following lines to the existing line of code:

```
$pos=particleShape1.position;
if ($pos.y<0)
particleShape1.lifespanPP=0;
```

Click on Edit and Close and then play the scene. Now when the particles fall below 0, they die. Be sure to keep the emitter placed above 0 in Y because that would restrict emission.

WORKING ON THE CHAIN GANG

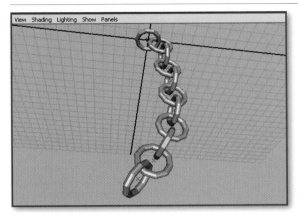

Helpful for rendering the latest rapper fashion accessories, here is an unusual use for rigid bodies. Start by choosing the option box for Create, Polygon Primitives, Torus. Change the Section Radius to .2 and the Subdivisions Around Axis and Height to 10. Make sure the radius is at 1, the twist is at 0, and the Axis is Y, and then press Create. Now, with pTorus1 selected, select the option box for Edit, Duplicate. Set the Number of Copies to 10 and make sure all options are unselected except for Copy and Parent. In the Translate box, enter 1.25, 0, 0 and in the Rotate, enter 90, 0, 0. Make sure Scale is 1 and press Duplicate. Now only select the original pTorus1 and choose Soft/Rigid Bodies, Create Passive Rigid Body. Now select all the other ones and choose Soft/Rigid Bodies, Active Rigid Bodies. While they are still selected, choose Fields, Gravity. Now play the scene, and you have a dangling chain.

   ## BATTLE TWO TURBULENCE FIELDS TOGETHER

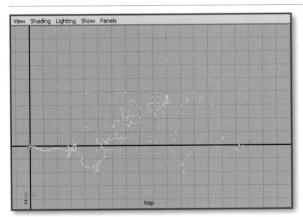

To really get rich and subtle effects with turbulence fields, use two of them with almost identical settings but slightly different frequencies and magnitudes. Then put opposite expressions in the Phase Field Attributes. For starters, try `phaseY=time* 3` in one turbulence field and `phaseY=time* -3.3`. This will cause the fields to interact and give you cool motion that you otherwise could not get with a single field.

   SWARMING BUGS OR ATTACHING FIELDS TO INDIVIDUAL PARTICLES

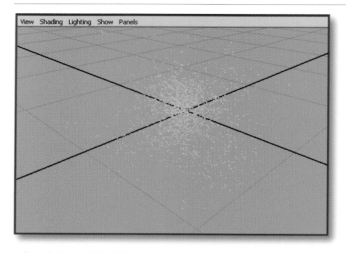

For your next massive bug attack movie, try this tip. Under the Particles menu, select Create Emitter options. Change it to an Omni with Speed set to 0 and Max Distance set to 1. Play the scene for 30 to 40 frames, but notice that there are particles emitted that are not moving at all. At this point, we want to freeze these particles in time and disconnect the emission. Select particle1 and then select Solvers, Initial State, Set for Selected. Next, in the Dynamics Relationships Editor, disconnect the emission. Do this by selecting particle1, and then, on the top right, select Emitters and click on emitter1 so that it becomes unhighlighted. Now when you rewind and play the scene, nothing happens, and the particles are idle. Select particle1 and then select Fields, Newton. Select both particle1 and newtonField1 and choose Fields, Use Selected as Source of Field. Now the field will be attached to each individual particle. In the newtonField1 Attribute Editor, select Apply Per Vertex under Special Effects. Now set the Magnitude to .1 and Attenuation to 0 under Newton Field Attributes. Last, make sure that Use Max Distance is unchecked. Set your timeline to be around 1000, hit play, and grab the bug repellant; you will need it.

MAKE A PARTICLE EMIT A TRAIL OF PARTICLES

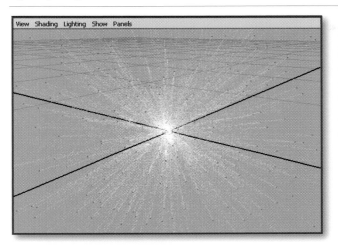

Let's use the bug swarm in the previous tip for this trick. Select particle1 to which we applied Newton Fields and choose the Particles, Emit from Object option box. Specify an Omni Emitter Type and press Create. Now if you play the scene, you will have particles all over that are not showing any trailing action. Select emitter2 that we just created and set the Speed to .1 under Attribute Editor, Basic Emission Speed Attributes. Next, choose particle2 and set the Lifespan Mode to Constant and the Lifespan value to .3 in its Attribute Editor. Next, go to the Add Dynamic Attributes section, select Opacity, and choose Add Per Particle Attribute. Right-click in opacityPP under Per Particle (Array) Attributes, choosing Create Ramp. Now right-click again in this field and select Edit Array Mapper. Change the Max Value from 1 to .2. Now change focus to the particleShape2 main attributes and under the Render Attributes, press the button that says Current Render Type and then change the Point Size to 1. Play the scene and experiment with different lifespans or add color with Add Dynamic Attributes, Color, Add Per Object Attributes for some cool effects.

  EMIT PARTICLES FROM AN IMAGE OR TEXTURE

Here is a cool tip for either surreal or practical uses. Create a horizontal NURBS plane and scale it to 30. With nurbsPlane1 selected, choose Particles, Emit from Object options. Change the emission type to be Surface. Select emitter1 and press Ctrl-A to get the Attribute Editor. Scroll down near the bottom to the area titled Texture Emission Attributes. Under the Texture Rate slider, press the radio button titled Enable Texture Rate. Next, press the button to the right of the Texture Rate slider. This will bring up the Create Render Node window that will enable you to choose what texture to use. For a quick check to see whether it is working, select the Checker pattern. Now particles will only emit from where the checker pattern is not black. In the emitter1 attributes, turn the Speed to 0 and then play the scene. You will see a checker pattern appear slowly with the particles. Turn up the amount of particles emitted to see the pattern better. To change the pattern, go into the attributes for the emitter, right-click on the Texture Rate attribute, and select Break Connection. Now you can add a different texture where the creative possibilities are quite endless, such as using an animated image map sequence.

KNOW YOUR FIELD OPTIONS

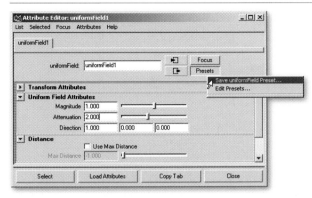

As you use dynamics increasingly, you may find you like to use certain settings as a starting point. It is useful to set up fields initially so that basic setup work can be avoided. Many of these settings are common to all fields and work the same regardless of the field. Here are the common ones: Magnitude is the strength of a field or how hard it pushes a particle. This setting depends on the scale of your scene, but it's useful to set this to 1 typically. Attenuation tones down the magnitude of a field with distance, similar to light decays. Setting this to 0 means that the field will affect the particles regardless of how near or far they are from the field. As you increase this value, the effect is localized around the field. Values from 1 to 2 are best, but you should start with 0. Also it is helpful to turn Max Distance off. Now as you create a field with these settings, you will have a good starting point. Disabling Max Distance and Attenuation will reduce potential confusion when you first add a field.

GET YOUR TURBULENCE ON

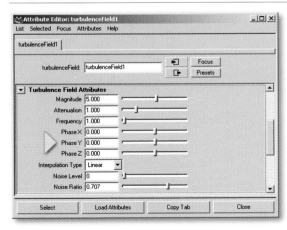

Adding a turbulence field to particles can create interesting and rich behaviors. Unfortunately, by default the turbulence pattern stays in place. Adding a simple expression on the Phase Y attribute will take care of this. Try `phaseY=time* 3` as a starting point. You will now see the pattern of the turbulence move with time. You can move the turbulence any direction you want using Phase X and Phase Z in combination with Phase Y. Often it is preferable to move the phase away or toward the camera if possible.

EMIT MORE PARTICLES AS THE EMITTER GOES FASTER

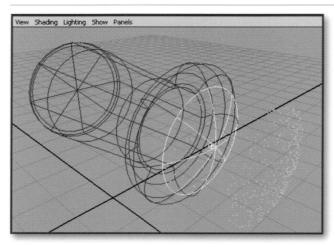

Here is a fairly advanced trick for which you may find a use. Maya typically does not let you vary emission rates with velocity, but this will enable such an effect. Create a sphere and add an expression to its translationX attribute, `tx=sin(time*3)`. As the scene is played, the ball should oscillate back and forth smoothly along X. With the ball selected, choose Particles, Emit from Object options, setting it as a Surface Emitter Type, setting the Rate (Particles/Sec) to 2000, and turning the speed to 0. In the particle1 Attribute Editor, turn Inherit Factor to 1 under Emission Attributes. Now under Lifespan Attributes, select lifespanPP only. Go down to the Per Particle (Array) Attributes, right-click on lifespanPP, and select Runtime Expression. Enter this expression:

```
$magv=mag(velocity);
if (rand(1)<linstep(0,1,$magv/3))
lifespanPP=1;
else
lifespanPP=0;
```

Now when you play the scene, you will see that the emission happens a lot more when the object is moving quickly. As the object slows down, very little emission takes place. To apply this to any other scene, you will need to know how fast the cutoff velocity is. To change that, change the numeral 3 under `$magv/3` to another integer value. The trick only works because Maya lets us see the inherited velocity in the Creation Expression. Perfect for salt-shaker or ketchup bottle animation!

PARTICLE REPLACEMENT

Here's an excellent part of the dynamics package that can really help with flocking move-ment of large groups of objects—particle geometry instancing. Basically a way to lynchpin instanced copies of objects to each particle, it is a great way to do flocks of birds, basic crowds, or falling boulders. The source object can be animated, or it can be a sequence of objects. Per particle attributes can enable individual modification of behavior, and different objects can be instanced to different particles. With a bit of ingenuity, many possibilities exist for complex animation when combined with the already rich particle toolset. To get started, create a simple primitive of your choice or hierarchical model if you like. Next, create a particle array with Particles, Particle Tool options set with Create Particle Grid checked, With Text Fields checked, and Minimum Corner set to –5, 0, –5 and Maximum Corner set to 5, 0, 5. After the particle array is created, select the object first, Ctrl-click to add the particle, and then choose Particles, Instancer (Replacement). Instance copies will now appear in place over each particle. Now, to make it interesting, apply some fields to the particle such as Air, Gravity, and Turbulence. Playback will be sluggish, so plan on playblasting frequently to evaluate the animation. Many creative options exist in the Instancer options menu, so delve in with fervor!

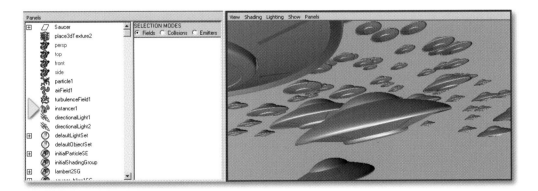

INVASION OF THE BLOB

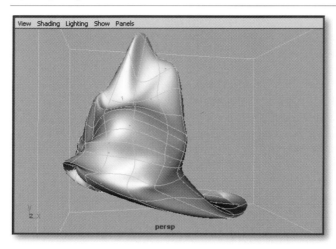

Soft bodies are one of the really fun and powerful features in Maya. A very simple but graphic demonstration of what they can do is an homage to the sci-fi classic *The Blob*. Start by creating a NURBS sphere with 16 spans and sections. Press "f" to fit the view. Right-click on the sphere and choose Materials, Assign New Material, Blinn. Change the color to .64, .80, .83 in RGB. Select the sphere and press 3 to increase screen resolution. In the dynamics menu, choose Soft/Rigid Bodies, Create Soft Body options and set Creation Options to Duplicate, Make Copy Soft, Hide Non-Soft Object, Make Non-Soft a Goal, and Weight of .7. Now go to Particles, Create Emitter options and set Type to Omni, Rate to 12, and Speed to 4. Open the particle1 Attribute Editor and set Render Attributes, Particle Render Type to Streak, Lifespan Mode to Constant with a Lifespan of .5 and Inherit Factor of 0. Set frame range to 100 and check for particle emission. Now with nothing selected, choose Fields, Air with settings of Magnitude 10, Speed 1, Direction XYZ all to 0, and Maximum Distance to 1. Now with airField1 and particle1 both selected, choose Fields, Use Selected As Source of Field. Open the Dynamic Relationships Editor and connect copyOfnurbsSphere1Particle to airField1. Now hit play and open the Attribute Editor for copyOfnurbsSphere1Particle. Nothing much happens until the Goal Weight for nurbsSphereShape1 is reduced from the default of .7 down lower. Blobby animation should begin, with many effects possible by altering Goal Smoothness, Emission Speed, and AirField Attenuation. Send out the government troops when necessary.

CACHE AND CACHE AGAIN

Normally, playback or playblasting of particle simulations is sufficient, but if scrubbing, playing in reverse, or clicking to an individual frame in the timeline is desired, run-up calculations can be output to disk or RAM cache. This can be used per object or scene-wise. For
individual particle objects to be cached to RAM, select the particle node and choose
Solvers, Memory Caching, Enable. Make sure Windows, Settings/Preferences, Preferences,
Dynamics, Run Up to Current Time is turned off. Play back sequence to load to cache, and
then when done with it, choose Solvers, Memory Caching, Delete. To write to disk, choose
Solvers, Create Particle Disk Cache. This method utilizes the cache even if additional fields
are added, so to disable it, choose Solvers, Edit Oversampling or Cache Settings and
uncheck Particle Disk Cache, Use Particle Disk Cache. If all this seems too involved for rou-
tine work, Maya offers easier run-up options in Window, Settings/Preferences, Preferences,
Settings, Dynamics with Run Up to Current Time options. By disabling this command,
dynamics will not be calculated if you need to scrub to check behavior of other non-
dynamic animation. The Save Startup Cache option also helps by saving a run-up cache in
your file, as opposed to on disk.

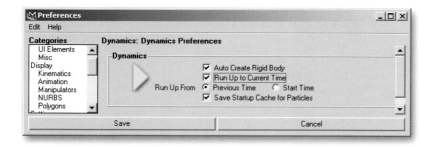

Getting Under the Hood

CUSTOMIZIN

mel

mel

model

ROTATI

SNAPPI

REAL WOR

PRODUCTI

GUI

Not to be confused with the cook at your local diner, MEL is the magic bullet in Maya. It is the ace in the hole, the joie de vive, the raison d'etre for Maya's

Getting Under the Hood
mud wrestling with MEL

By Erick Miller, Contributor

existence. As for your existence, it makes life simultaneously easier and more difficult—it enables you to get under the hood and tweak to your heart's content, and it tempts you to spend endless hours doing so. The only catch is that there is a big bouncer at the door—the challenge of getting familiar with a programming language. Learning MEL in one chapter of an introductory book is not exactly a reasonable task, so this chapter will aim at those who are already underway in their exploration of the subject. If the bouncer doesn't seem too intimidating, it is certainly worth the time as the real unbridled power of Maya becomes yours. Unfortunately, only you will know of the massive powers you will wield, as your non-CG friends may not exactly see it that way.

   HUH? USING *WHATIS* AND *HELP*

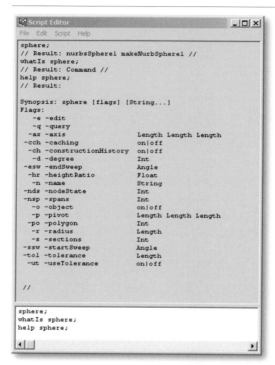

When getting started with MEL scripting, you will have many questions running through your head. Besides constantly consulting the software manuals, there are a couple really useful MEL commands that were specifically designed to "help" users figure things out. First, the command `whatIs` can tell you exactly what any MEL-related thing is. If Maya can recognize it as either a variable, command, or MEL script that exists in its internal memory, then it will identify to you what it is. Let's start with a command that we can recognize: `sphere`. By typing the command **sphere** in the Script Editor, we can create a NURBS sphere. But what if we had not known what sphere was or what it did? How could we quickly and easily find out? Well, we could simply ask Maya to tell us by typing:

whatIs sphere;

Maya will happily tell us what it is: a command. Now that we know we're looking at a command, we can find out even more information by using the `help` command. Asking for help is simple. If we type **help sphere**, Maya will tell us all the information, including command line flags and syntax, that it has registered about the usage of the `sphere` command. Note that the `help` command only works with commands and doesn't know about MEL keywords like `if` or `while`. Regardless, using `whatIs` and `help` can still be useful when trying to figure things out, especially during those times when you can use all the help you can get!

VARIABLES AND *EVAL* THIS, *EVAL* THAT

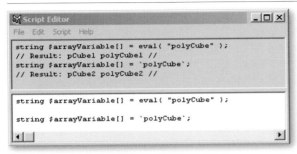

Variables are, to put it simply, the places where you put data while your script is running. They are little storage cans into which you can stuff whatever you want dynamically. So, how do you get data from one location into a variable in your own MEL script? Well, first off, you only really need to know one simple thing—you "get" data by evaluating a procedure that "returns" the data into your variable. What, you may ask, is the data that is returned? Well, it doesn't matter what the data is. That's the whole point of having variables—they can contain pretty much anything you want. However, you do need to know that the data type of the variable does matter, and once you know that, you can start using variables to their full potential. Let's use the `polyCube` command as an example. The `polyCube` command makes a polygon cube and returns the names of the nodes that it made in a string array. If a command returns some data of a specific type, that means you can put it in a variable of matching type, just like this:

```
string $arrayVariable[] = eval( "polyCube" );
```

Or, alternatively, back ticks will evaluate a command as well:

```
string $arrayVariable[] = `polyCube`;
```

In either example, if you print the contents of `$arrayVariable`, you will get the array of names of the cube nodes that were created, pCube1 polyCube1.

ACTING CONDITIONALLY

Conditions are really just ways of making decisions based on a series of prerequisites. Sort of like a filter in your code, a conditional statement can keep certain things from happening and make other things happen instead if the condition tests to be true or false. There are a few different ways of writing a conditional statement, but the most common is by using the keywords `if`, `else`, and `else if`. Another cool way of writing a condition is by using a `switch` statement with `case` statements. The final, most cryptic but space-efficient way is by using the `?` `:` operators. The one thing to remember about conditions is this: A conditional statement is simply testing for true or false. This means that anything put into a condition must either evaluate to zero or one—and if it evaluates to one (in effect, true), then the condition tests as positive, and therefore that portion of code is executed. To be or not to be? Well, in a MEL script, it's based on the condition!

```
M Script Editor                                           _ |□| X|
File   Edit   Script   Help

;
THE CAR IS RED!
This vehicle has 4 wheels

string $vehicle = "car";
string $color = "red";
int $wheels = 4;

if( $vehicle == "car" )
{
        switch( $color )
        {
                case "red" :
                        print "THE CAR IS RED!\n";
                        break;
                case "blue" :
                        print "THE CAR IS BLUE!\n";
                        break;
                default:
                        print ("THE CAR IS "+$color+"!\n");
        }
}
else if( $vehicle == "truck" )
{
        print "THE VEHICLE IS A TRUCK!\n";
}
else
{
        print ("THE VEHICLE IS"+$vehicle+"\n!");
}

print (($wheels!=4) ? "This vehicle needs some repair\n" : "This vehicle has 4 wheels\n" );
```

THE SHEER EXCITEMENT OF ARRAY VARIABLES

```
Script Editor                          _ □ ×
File  Edit  Script  Help
string $array[];
$array[0] = "one";
// Result: one //
$array[1] = "two";
// Result: two //
$array[2] = "three";
// Result: three //
$array[ `size $array` - 1 ] = "four";
// Result: four //
clear( $array );
// Result: 0 //

string $array[];

$array[0] = "one";
$array[1] = "two";
$array[2] = "three";
$array[ `size $array` - 1 ] = "four";

clear( $array );
```

Need to store a big list of stuff? Then an array is just right for you. Arrays are dynamically growing data structures in MEL; you can have arrays of many different data types—integers, floats, strings, and vectors. Unfortunately, you can't have an array of matrices, but that's probably all right. Using arrays is quite simple and can be very useful. Let's say you need to write a script that puts an unknown amount of string data into a list in order to keep track of things. Well, using an array to store everything is the thing to do. You can start using arrays by simply assigning data to each element in the list; for example:

```
string $array[ ];
$array[ 0]  = "one";
$array[ 1]  = "two";
$array[ 2]  = "three";
```

You can then dynamically add new elements into the array by using the `size` command and indexing the array using the current size minus one, like this:

```
$array[ `size $array`-1]  = "four";
```

One important thing to remember about arrays in MEL is that they are the only data type that is passed by reference—that means that if you pass an array into a MEL procedure, the procedure has the capability to directly modify the contents of the array that you just passed into it. This is so that Maya does not have to make an entire copy of the array in memory just to pass the data around from one procedure to another. Finally, you can delete all the contents of your array by using the `clear` command. To completely destroy an array from memory, simply type:

```
clear( $array );
```

DOING THE LOOP

```
Script Editor                                    _ |□| x|
File  Edit  Script  Help
int $intArray[] = { 0, 1, 2, 3, 4, 5, 6, 7, 8, 9, 10 };
for( $elem in $intArray )
{
       print ( "Array Element  " + $elem + "\n" );
}
;
Array Element  0
Array Element  1
Array Element  2
Array Element  3
Array Element  4
Array Element  5
Array Element  6
Array Element  7
Array Element  8
Array Element  9
Array Element  10

int $intArray[] = { 0, 1, 2, 3, 4, 5, 6, 7, 8, 9, 10 };
int $i = 0;
while( $i <= 5 )
{
       print ($intArray[$i]+ " is less than equal to 5...\n");
       $i++;
};
0 is less than equal to 5...
1 is less than equal to 5...
2 is less than equal to 5...
3 is less than equal to 5...
4 is less than equal to 5...
5 is less than equal to 5...
```

```
int $intArray[] = { 0, 1, 2, 3, 4, 5, 6, 7, 8, 9, 10 };
for( $elem in $intArray )
{
       print ( "Array Element  " + $elem + "\n" );
}

int $intArray[] = { 0, 1, 2, 3, 4, 5, 6, 7, 8, 9, 10 };
int $i = 0;
while( $i <= 5 )
{
       print ($intArray[$i]+ " is less than equal to 5...\n");
       $i++;
```

What is a loop? Well, it's not a dance, although it may feel like one when you are done! A loop is an extremely useful way of cycling over lists of data or building up lists of data. A loop is usually either a way to process the contents of an array or a way to repeatedly execute a set of commands in order to build an array. Sometimes, though, it is useful to execute a bunch of commands over and over again without returning data until a certain condition is met that tells us that it is ok to stop. There are two different keywords for writing loops in MEL, `for` and `while`. Here is a simple example of using a `for` loop:

```
int $intArray[] = {  0, 1, 2,
➡3, 4, 5, 6, 7, 8, 9, 10 };
for( $elem in $intArray )
{
print ( "Array Element  " +
➡$elem + "\n" );
}
```

And here is an example of using a `while` loop:

```
int $intArray[] = {  0, 1, 2, 3, 4, 5, 6, 7, 8, 9, 10 };
int $i = 0;
while( $i <= 5 )
{
       print ($intArray[ $i] + "is less than 5...\n");
       $i++;
}
```

WRITING CUSTOM PROCEDURES

```
Script Editor                                    _|□|x|
File  Edit  Script  Help

global proc string exampleProcedure( string $arg )
{
      //
      // any custom logic goes here:
            string $variable = "The string I passed in is: "+$arg;
            return ( $variable );
}
```

There comes a time in everyone's life when regular MEL just isn't enough, when custom logic is needed that MEL doesn't offer right out of the box. When that time comes, writing a custom procedure can answer all your needs. Writing a procedure in MEL enables you to define your own arguments, create your own block of logic, and then return the values that you have calculated as data that can be stored in other variables and used from within other scripts. If written generically and in enough of a multi-purpose fashion, sometimes your custom procedures can even be reused continuously by yourself or others. So, let's break down a custom procedure.

```
global proc string exampleProcedure( string $arg )
{
//
// any custom logic goes here:
string $variable = "The string I passed in is: "+$arg;
return ( $variable );
}
```

First, the keyword `global` tells Maya that what you are declaring should be available to the rest of Maya as a global function. Next, the keyword `proc` tells Maya that you are declaring a procedure. Next, the keyword `string` basically says that this procedure is going to return some data and is defining the data type that will be returned as a string. Next is the name of the procedure, which can be anything you like, and enclosed within parentheses are the arguments to the procedure—what the input must be for the procedure to run. Finally, within the brackets, known as scope operators, you can put whatever logic you want. When you are done writing your custom logic, all you need to do is return the answer using the `return` statement. Just make sure that the data type of the data you are returning is the same type as what is declared at the beginning of the function. You can then use your custom procedure in another script by first making sure you source the script that contains the custom procedure and then doing something like the following:

```
string $fun = "this is fun";
string $value = 'exampleProcedure $fun';
```

OOPS: *WARNING, ERROR,* AND *CATCH*

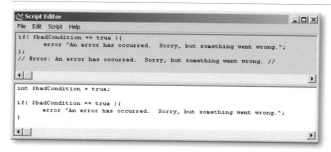

Sometimes planning for errors is just as much a part of the script writing process as writing the actual script. Adding additional code to handle certain cases that might cause errors is a process known as error handling. One really easy way to notify you that an error has occurred inside of your code before anything really bad happens is by using the MEL command `error`. The `error` command will immediately exit from your script and display a red error message in the Script Editor output. Creating an `if` statement that will be entered into when an error occurs is probably the most common way of using the `error` command:

```
if( $badCondition == true ){
        error "An error has occurred.   Sorry, but something went wrong.";
}
```

If you encounter a situation that's not an error, but there is still potential that a problem may occur, then try using the `warning` command. The `warning` command is similar to the `error` command in that it prints a colored message at the bottom of the screen to alert the user, but `warning` does not cause the script to fatally exit. Instead, `warning` continues to execute the rest of the script after it is called. We don't like errors and prefer Maya to continue generally, which is what the `catch` command is for. Anywhere in your code where you think you might encounter an error that isn't *really* an error is a good place to use the `catch` command. A good example of this would be deleting all cameras in your scene, but Maya gives you an error if you do that because it just won't let you delete the very last default camera. You could add extra logic to check for that, or you could simply wrap the `delete` command with a `catch`:

```
//
// FORCE DELETE ALL CAMERAS IN THE SCENE ->
//
string $cameras[] = 'ls -type camera'
for($cam in $cameras)
{
camera -e -sc false $cam;
}
catch('delete $cameras');
```

So, if you want your script to error out, use the `error` command; if you know there will be an error, and you want your script to keep on executing, then use the `catch` command.

USING *CREATENODE, NODETYPE,* AND *LS*

Pretty much everything that's useful in Maya is represented by a node. To list all the node types in Maya, you can print out the results from the ever-so-useful `ls` command:

```
print 'ls -nodeTypes';
```

You'll see that this yields a really long list. But, say you need to create a node of a particular type in your script—*how do you do that*? It's simple: Use the `createNode` command and pass it the node type that you want to create:

```
createNode plusMinusAverage;
```

The preceding command creates a single math utility node of type *plusMinusAverage*. All node types that exist in Maya can be created this way and will be initialized in their default state. This is a useful thing to know because sometimes you don't want to jump through hoops just to create a simple node. Also, you might want to find out what the type of a node is that already exists in your scene. This is also a simple matter of calling a single command, called `nodeType`, and passing in the name of the node whose type you would like to query. Let's say we create a NURBS sphere from the Create menu. If we then want to find out what the type is for the NURBS shape node, we can call the following command:

```
nodeType nurbsSphereShape1;
// Result: nurbsSurface //
```

The text nurbsSphereShape1 is the name of the shape node of the sphere that we just created. The result of this command is a string that represents the node type; in this case, the result is nurbsSurface, which is the generic node type that represents all NURBS surfaces in Maya. So remember: If it is a node, then it has a corresponding type.

  ADDING, GETTING, SETTING, AND CONNECTING ATTRIBUTES

Attributes in Maya can be incredibly useful as a general way either to store data or to pass data from one node to another. MEL exposes many ways to control attributes, from creating them to getting, setting, and connecting them. To create an attribute, use the MEL command `addAttr`. First, select an object that you want to add the attribute onto and execute this:

```
addAttr -ln myCustomAttribute -at double;
```

To set your newly created attribute's keyable property to true (so that it shows up in the Channel Box and can be keyframed), use the MEL command `setAttr`:

```
setAttr -e -keyable true .myCustomAttribute;
```

You can also use `setAttr` to set actual attribute values:

```
setAttr .myCustomAttribute 2.25;
```

If you need to get the value of an attribute, you can use the MEL command `getAttr`:

```
getAttr .myCustomAttribute;
// Result: 2.25 //
```

Finally, if you want to connect two attributes together so that your newly created attribute controls another attribute, you can use the `connectAttr` command:

```
connectAttr .myCustomAttribute .translateY;
```

Now the custom attribute that you created is controlling the `translateY` attribute of the transform node that it was added to.

ARRAY ATTRIBUTE OR ATTRIBUTE ARRAY?

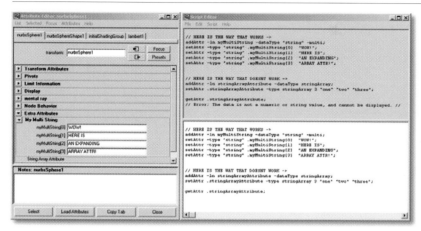

You might think that you could easily create an array of string attributes on a node for storing a list of strings. Both beginning and experienced MEL scripters will find they instead need to have a string array attribute. After reading the MEL addAttr documentation, they will try to add an attribute that is of data type stringArray, like this:

```
addAttr -ln stringArrayAttribute -dataType stringArray;
```

Inevitably, they will be plagued with an error because the attribute is a complex data type, which is likely not what you want if having a simple array of strings that you can easily get and set from within MEL is your goal.

All attributes can be made into an array, regardless of their type, by using a single flag in the addAttr command! This means that Maya creates a distinction between the data types of attributes and the capability to create multiple elements as an attribute array. The option of calling an attribute a multi attribute is Maya's way of saying it can be expanded into an array of multiple attributes. After you make an attribute a multi, you can then refer to its elements by using the standard array index operators—for example, [0], [1], [2].... Here is an example of creating a multi attribute and then automatically expanding that attribute into an array using setAttr:

```
addAttr -ln myMultiString -dataType "string" -multi;
setAttr -type "string" .myMultiString[ 0]   "WOW!";
setAttr -type "string" .myMultiString[ 1]   "HERE IS";
setAttr -type "string" .myMultiString[ 2]   "AN EXPANDING";
setAttr -type "string" .myMultiString[ 3]   "ARRAY ATTR!";
```

It works with any attribute type you give it, including doubles, ints, and so on. The first attempted method doesn't work because the data of an attribute that is of data type stringArray is storing an entire array all in one attribute, not individually as separate elements. Because Maya has deemed these string array attribute data types to be considered "complex" data, it does not yet have a mechanism in MEL for performing getAttr on them.

Real World Production

REAL WORLD
PRODUCTION

Ah, the wild and woolly world of effects production. The saying goes that a CG artist spends half his or her life trying to get into it and the other half trying to get

Real World Production Methods

otherwise known as stress

out of it. It is definitely an acquired taste, where some have a stomach for the stress and technical challenges, and some may end up bartending or selling real estate. Either way, it is both an exhilarating and exhausting career, full of headaches and small victories along the way. To minimize the headache component, this chapter is written to provide a checklist for the final rendering phase, which is where most of the stress occurs, where the rubber meets the road and the chicken crosses it (or something like that). It can be maddening or pleasant, and I have found that these little nuggets of cheap advice save my stockpile of Excedrin from dwindling. In the end, CG production is an insatiable drive that manifests itself such that as one project fades onto the rental shelf, the ambition to pioneer CG history again renews itself. One thing we CG artists do not lack is the motivation to explore new ground.

     TAMING THE RAM BEAST

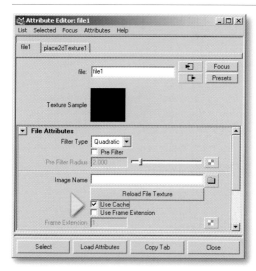

RAM concerns present themselves when working with the Maya renderer, or any renderer for that matter. Maya tends to use lots of RAM, so here are some handy tricks for reducing the load. The tip in Chapter 5 entitled, "Determining Texture Resolution," should get you a long way initially. Next, under a File Texture's File Attributes, there is a check box for Use Cache. This will write textures to a hard disk cache until needed in the render, as opposed to storing everything in RAM as normal. To really take advantage of this technique, though, convert all textures to the BOT (block ordered textures) file type. Use "`maya -optimizeRender original_file.mb optimized_file.mb`" in a shell to auto-matically create BOT files for all textures in your scene. Similar to RenderMan's .tex format, it creates a proper mip-map or nesting of power of two resamples within one file, letting the renderer select the nearest one to a given screen space. This lowers RAM, speeds caching, and chooses properly screen-sized resolutions, which leads to much better anti-aliasing of textures. Also try to keep textures at a square aspect ratio at powers of two, such as 128, 256, 512, 1k, 2k, 4k, and so on. This can often fix problems such as not enough sharpness in the map or too much sharpness and resultant aliasing. The last option to reduce RAM usage is the `-tw` and `-th` Tile Height option flags in the command line renderer. You can choose a smaller tile size such as 64 that will load less geometry at a time. Lastly, one can save smaller versions of maps that you use while working to speed things up and then replace them with the hi-res version when you are doing finals.

MINIMIZING TEXTURE ALIASING

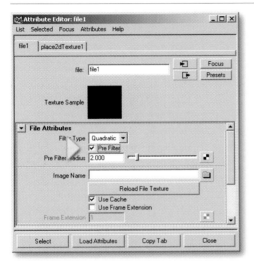

Aliasing is another of the sore spots with the Maya renderer, so these tips will help to alleviate this frustrating behavior. First, render two or three frames to check the temporal aliasing as a matter of habit; it will be impossible to see in a single frame. Using properly-sized texture maps and BOT formats as discussed in the previous tip will get you pretty far to begin with. If problems persist, increase the Filter amount in the File Texture File Attributes if you have set it to less than one. Maya now defaults to Quadratic as the base filter type, which is a bit more expensive, but the expense is worth the results. Two pre- and post-filter options exist for the really tough ones. Use the Pre Filter check box below the Filter Type pull-down to soften the map before calculation. In the Render Globals, the Multi-pixel Filtering option will soften the entire image as a global solution. Use of square power of two textures as mentioned in the previous tip will help, as well as making sure the aliasing is not coming from excessive bump map settings.

PRE AND POST MEL

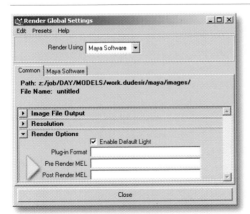

Under Render Globals, Render Options there exists a handy set of functions—Pre Render MEL and Post Render MEL. As an example, this enables the application of custom render preset settings, hiding or unhiding of objects, and so on during rendering and restoring back afterward. With a bit of crafty coding, perhaps an email or a phone dialing can be set up for render completion notification.

LOCK DOWN THOSE SHADOWS

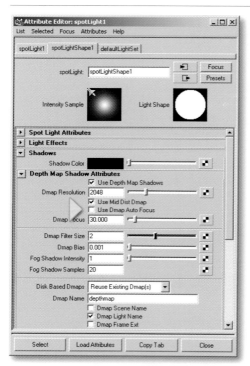

Another infuriating result from an overnight render can be unstable shadow maps, resulting in pops, slides, and artifacts. Part of the problem is native to shadow map technique, and some of it is due to Maya's implementation, but these tips will help lock them down. First, turn off Dmap Auto Focus in the shadow map attributes, adjusting the angle manually to match the cone angle. This feature attempts to optimize a shadow map's application, but it often brings in instability. Next, increase Dmap Filter Size for softer edge roping, but be careful of increases in render time. Next, use the Reuse Existing Dmaps option for static shadows. Lastly and most importantly, check that Auto Render Clip Plane is turned off in the Camera Attribute Editor and that clipping is bound to the model's extents and not exceeding the 0.1 to 20,000 ratio.

GENERAL SPEED IMPROVEMENT

People have observed that rendering times have remained constant over the years, even as processor speeds go through the roof and RAM becomes as cheap as French fries (as a friend once noted). So, speed optimization is always welcome and relevant. In NURBS modeling, examine the models for degree 3 surfaces where degree 1 can suffice. Check revolves for excessive sections and intermediate wasted CVs. Check for manually set Advanced Tessellation over automatic settings. In poly models, look for overly high resolution meshes and pieces that can be combined. In lighting, avoid Area lights and shadow-casting Point lights. Reuse shadow maps if possible or paint them into textures. In shading, convert solid textures to 2D maps with Convert To File Texture. Lastly, use glows sparingly because these can equal the render time of geometry.

REDUCING MOTION BLUR ARTIFACTS

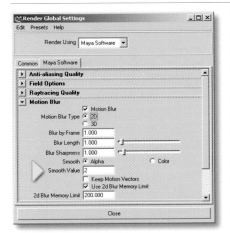

Motion blur problems are another fact of life in 3D rendering. Here are a few tips to help. As with any artifacting, check camera clipping first and turn off Auto Render Clip Plane as mentioned in the tip earlier in the chapter entitled, "Lock Down Those Shadows." If using 3D motion blur, individual object problems can be sampled higher than usual in Attribute Editor, Render Stats, Shading Samples Override. 3D motion blur has inherent problems with shadow maps, so shadows may need to be painted, or 2D motion blur may be used. With 2D motion blur, rendering with the post process of "blur2d" (described in the tip, "Motion Blur Choices," in Chapter 6, "From Home Movies to Hollywood: Camerawork Basics") can control the output without requiring a re-render. One common artifact of 2D motion blur is a white halo surrounding objects. Make sure that your background is black and that there is no environmental fog in the scene. Another fix that can help is to set the Smooth Value to 0 in the Render Global Motion Blur attributes, or try reversing the Smooth Alpha/Color option.

CHECK YOUR RELEASE NOTES

One area of the documentation many Maya artists may overlook is the Release Notes. Previously issued as separate text files, they are now integrated in the general help HTML page. The purpose of Release Notes is to state known limitations or workarounds for unique problems that other users have encountered in their work. They are generally issues that may get a bug fix in upcoming releases, or perhaps they are general limitations of the package. Either way, a workaround is offered that may or may not rectify the problem. Overall, though, they are very useful to consult during sticky problems or when a new release is made to see the potholes ahead in the road.

SETTING UP MATTES

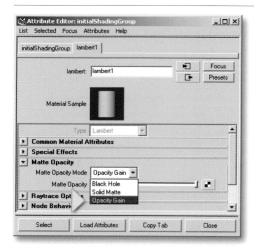

Typically in production, separate layers are rendered, as opposed to having everything rendered in camera. The tip entitled "Layer It On" in Chapter 5 covers how to set up the basic breakdown of layers. Often though, a compositor may request a matte render for a particular element embedded in one of these layers. Maya provides some excellent shader-centric tools for this task, located under the Matte Opacity menu in a shader's Attribute Editor. Matte Opacity is a basic control to reduce the amount of alpha contribution to the alpha channel or a render, allowing for the partial or full removal of objects in the comp. More useful, though, is the Matte Opacity Mode pull-down, giving three choices for matte behavior of an element. The default Opacity Gain allows a variable amount as just mentioned. Solid Matte differs in that a constant value is used for the matte, overriding any partial transparency. Black Hole is very useful for knocking out full mattes because it zeroes out any matte contribution for any object behind, leaving a clean matte removal. Lastly, mattes can be created by using a black background color and a white incandescence value on the shader to achieve certain effects. With a bit of ingenuity, matte combinations can provide anything you need.

 ## RENDER DIAGNOSTICS

Even though you may have done your render setup homework properly, Maya provides an automated check that reports some basic problems or recommendations for an optimal render. You can locate it in Render, Render Diagnostics. It reports findings in categories of Known Problems/Limitations, Warnings, and Speed/Memory Implications. It will not, however, recommend that you extract your head from the monitor, get outdoors more often, and exercise, but that would be a useful diagnostic for any Maya artist.

178 **CHAPTER 10** • Real World Production Methods

Z DEPTH RENDERS

Another frequently rendered layer useful in production is that of the Z depth pass. This is commonly used by compositors for a variety of functions, from establishing depth of field to desaturating over distance to atmospheric cueing. Similar to shadow map file types, a Z depth file is a non-graphic high bit depth indexing of depth calculations. It can be viewed as a grayscale image, however, by using Fcheck and using the "z" key to view. Not all image file formats embed the Z channel though, so Maya will often write it to a separate file in that case. Be sure that your compositing package can accept the format you choose because the files are always proprietary in format. Lastly, a cheap alternative to true depth maps is to use a depth shader, found online on Highend3d.com. It simply sets a grayscale range through the depth of the entire model, so that the Z depth is effectively your render. The tradeoff is that you only end up with 256 levels of depth versus the more extensive amount resident in depth maps.

RENDERING LARGER THAN 8K

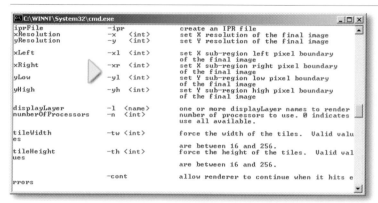

It seems there is always someone out there wondering how to create a rendering for a 5' x 10' poster at 300 dpi. This is generally a bad idea because higher dpi's are normally set for small print work, not billboards. However, there are occasional uses for very large renders for illustration work or fine art. Maya tops out at an 8k×8k resolution, so if more resolution is desired, here is a clever workaround. In the command-line render options, there exist flags for x and y resolution but also for sub-regions of the overall field (xLeft, xRight, yHigh, yLow). Maya only cares about the 8k limit for its current render, so by breaking up a render into smaller sub-region components, it can be assembled in a paint package to the full resolution. So, for a 10,000×5,000 pixel render, the usage command for the two would be:

```
Render -x 10000 -y 5000 -xl 0 -xr 5000 -yl 0 -yh 5000 -p first_piece
scene.mb
Render -x 10000 -y 5000 -xl 5001 -xr 10000 -yl 0 -yh 5000 -p second_piece
scene.mb
```

A FINAL RENDER CHECKLIST

As a summary of some of the many tips in this book, here is a checklist I use frequently before an expensive overnight render at the eleventh hour of a project, along with throwing a chicken bone over my left shoulder and dancing around in circles for good luck:

- Is all geometry as optimal as possible (no wasted, flat, or excessive CVs or faces)?
- Is NURBS tessellation all set to Advanced and adjusted to screen space?
- Is camera clipping not exceeding a 0.1 to 20,000 ratio?
- Is Auto Render Clip Plane turned off in the camera attributes?
- Is bump-mapping depth set around .1 to .2 versus 1?
- Are all file texture filter values set to at least 1?
- Has a test render of two to three frames been done to check texture aliasing?
- Is Reuse Shadow Maps used for static shadows?
- Is Dmap Auto Focus turned off and set manually in spotlight shadows?
- Are all history and construction curves deleted?
- Has File, Optimize Scene Size been done?
- Has Multilister, Edit, Delete Unused been done?
- Are BOT textures used?
- Are textures sampled down to screen space and at powers of two?
- Is animation padding set to 4?
- Do you feel lucky today?

INDEX

informIT

www.informit.com